Deeper

Still

Deeper Still

By

Janice Leasure Woodrum

DESTINY IMAGE® PUBLISHERS, INC.
P.O. Box 310, Shippensburg, PA 17257-0310
"Promoting Inspired Lives."

This book and all other Destiny Image and Destiny Image Fiction books are available at Christian bookstores and distributors worldwide.

For more information on foreign distributors, call
717-532-3040.
Or reach us on the Internet: www.destinyimage.com

ISBN 13 TP: 978-0-7684-4333-2
ISBN 13 eBook: 978-0-7684-4334-9

For Worldwide Distribution, Printed in the U.S.A.
1 2 3 4 5 6 7 8 9 10 11 /23 22 21 20 19 18

Dedication

This book is dedicated to my dear friends, Ralph and Cathy. Your lives have been a clear reflection to me of the Savior's abundant love, His power to bring restoration and fullness of life into broken places, and His victorious spirit of holiness and perseverance through times of misrepresentation and persecution. You are a living demonstration of the truth of God's life, and His powerful and holy ways as found in the following scripture passages:

"My grace if sufficient for you, for my power is made perfect in weakness. Therefore I will boast all the more gladly about my weaknesses, so that Christ's power may rest on me. That is why, for Christ's sake, I delight in weaknesses, in insults, in hardships, in persecutions, in difficulties. For when I am weak, then I am strong"

2 Cor.12:9-10 NIV.

"Then those who feared the Lord spoke to one another, and the Lord listened and heard them; so a book of remembrance was written before Him for those who fear the Lord and who meditate on His name. 'They shall be Mine' says the Lord of hosts, 'on the day that I make them My jewels. And I will spare them as a man spares his own son who serves him.' "

Malachi 3:16-17 NKJV

Table of Contents

Introduction

In this place of semi-confinement, I searched for reading material that I could digest in small increments and find morsels of strength and encouragement for my soul, as my body slowly healed from a head injury. It was then that the red paperback version of a forty-year-old masterpiece caught my eye. How many times had I read it over the years? I could not recount. But I picked it up like an old friend to comfort and commiserate with me in my discomfort and forced departure from my usual busy schedule.

Slowly and carefully finding my way back to the old recliner that had become both chair and bed in these days of recovery, my mind flashed back to the first time I read this book.

It was in the late 1970's and we were stationed in Landstuhl, West Germany in the U.S. Army. From this base we often made short trips over weekends or holidays to explore some other parts of Germany or the surrounding European countries.

One of our earlier explorations was made with several others who were friends of ours. We departed from what had become a pleasant and safe haven in West Germany, and made our way slowly by night train – destination Berlin. In those days the wall separating West Germany from East Germany was very real, strong and tangibly ominous. United States passports in hand, we made the eerie nighttime inspection and crossing, and proceeded on into this seemingly abandoned and "forbidden" territory. Berlin was hidden deep inside the heart of East Germany.

And truly the land itself was nearly forbidden. Only the city of Berlin itself was open to travelers from the West. For in a strange political compromise at the end of World War II, Berlin became the property of both the East and the West sections of Germany. There a very high and seemingly insurmountable concrete wall divided the two parts of the city, and forbade casual traffic from West to East or East to West.

The Germans were not afforded any opportunity to cross the forbidden barriers, and some people had no hopes of ever seeing family members who lived only a few kilometers away on the opposite side. But some foreign travelers were permitted to cross over to visit the mysterious and intriguing East side and return again to the West. This was the quest and rather nervous anticipation of our little group.

But in the course of preparation to make the exciting journey into "the East," we made a sad discovery. My passport was issued by the U.S. Army shortly before our departure from the U.S. for our three year stint in Germany. And with this distinctive marking, it would disqualify me from making the crossing to the East. So only the other seven people in our group could go. Sadly, I alone would spend the day in our hotel to pass the hours until the group's return late that evening.

But in my disappointment, Father God had a "consolation prize" for me of immense and unforgettable proportions. By His hand, a small paperback book had made its way into someone's baggage, and it was placed into my hands to accompany me in the long hours of that fateful day when I was "left behind" in a strange and formidable city deep within an almost impenetrable country. I had no clue what a marvelous and terrible journey awaited me.

The stunning and captivating book, *The Hiding Place* was not yet ten years old, having been copyrighted in 1971. As the others departed for their exciting adventure, I curled up in the gigantic German bed of our hotel room, and pulled the featherbed* up around me.

*A featherbed of this kind is a heavy down-filled comforter.

"Can you fathom the mysteries of God? Can you probe the limits of the Almighty? They are higher than the heavens – what can you do? They are deeper than the depths of the grave – what can you know? Their measure is longer than the earth and wider than the sea."

Job 11:7-9

Chapter One

Beneath The Featherbed

My experience there in that big bed in the hotel in Berlin was similar to that of Joni Eareckson Tada, who wrote the forward of the current new edition of **The Hiding Place**, printed in 2005. And that day in Berlin, it was also "just the story I needed to hear." Here is her comment:

> "The first chapter had me hooked. Although Corrie was from a different era, her life reached across the decades. World War II was far different from my own holocaust, but her ability to look straight into the terrifying jaws of a gas-chambered hell and walk out courageously into the sunshine of the other side was – well, just the story I needed to hear."[1]

That day, as the others nervously made the tenuous border crossing and explored the black and white starkness of the city of East Berlin, I explored in the pages of Corrie ten Boom's book, a gruesome tour into an era that closed near the time I was born – 1948. I believe this little book that serendipitously made its way into my hands that day, gave me a far deeper glimpse into the circumstances behind the division between East and West Germany, and the reason we as U.S. Army personnel occupied bases in the West.

Corrie's book describes her life, working happily in the family's watch repair shop in Holland, who during the atrocities of the Second World War was taken captive and placed in a concentration camp in Germany, along with her father and siblings. Several siblings were soon released, as it was discovered they were not closely involved in the forbidden practice of "hiding Jews" in their homes, in order to help them escape the Nazi torture and extermination camps during the holocaust of World War II. Corrie's father, in fragile health and advanced in age, didn't last long in the stark environment. Only Corrie and her sister Betsie remained for the long and torturous months ahead. But Betsie's fragile physical constitution didn't fare well in the stark, very cold and inhumane environment.

Finally, after many months, with advanced pneumonia, Betsie was moved from the barracks to a "hospital" of sorts, which in reality was barely more than a "holding pattern" until death finally took its inevitable course.

During Corrie and Betsie's long season together in captivity, Betsie was almost always the stronger in her faith, retaining her deep trust in God amidst the horrendous and dismal circumstances of the concentration camps. As Betsie was being transferred to the hospital acutely ill, she and Corrie shared what turned out to be their last exchange of precious words. Even in her very severely compromised state, Betsie tried desperately to console her sister at their time of parting.

At that moment Betsie's historic and indestructible words to Corrie on their parting were these:

"...must tell people what we have learned here. We must tell them that *there is no pit so deep that He is not deeper still.* They will listen to us, Corrie, because we have been here."[2]

Corrie was not allowed to come and visit her sister, but only waved at her for a few moments several times over the next few days through a filthy and cloudy window...and then she was gone.

After Betsie's death Corrie was allowed to see her briefly, piled in a row with other corpses, along a dark back wall of the hospital. Corrie describes her experience in *The Hiding Place.*[2]

"I raised my eyes to Betsie's face. 'Lord Jesus – what have You done? Oh Lord, what are You saying? What are You giving me?' "

For there lay Betsie, her eyes closed as if in sleep, her face full and young. The care lines, the grief lines, the deep hollows of hunger and disease were simply gone. In front of me was the Betsie of Haarlem (Holland), happy and at peace. Stronger! Freer! This was the Betsie of Haarlem, bursting with joy and health. Even her hair was graciously in place as if an angel had ministered to her."

Her life and death had proven her own words so unmistakably true, *"...there is no pit so deep that He is not deeper still."*

And now, from my place of recovery from my accident and head injury, I have found great solace in Paul's wise words to the Corinthians in 2 Corinthians 4:7-11:

*"But we have this treasure in jars of clay to show that this all-surpassing power is from God and not from us. We are **hard pressed on every side, but not crushed; perplexed, but not in despair; persecuted, but not abandoned; struck down, but not destroyed**. We always carry around in our body the death of Jesus, so that the life of Jesus may also be revealed in our body. For we who are alive are always being given over to death for Jesus' sake, so that His life may be revealed in our mortal body."*

Suddenly in my spirit I realized that the "deeper still" of Betsie's last words to Corrie were somehow described in this brief passage that has been largely a mystery to me these thirty-nine years since I received Jesus Christ as my personal Lord and Savior.

I have read this passage so many times, and passed over it without taking a deeper look into what I am discovering to be the "deeper still" described by the wise suffering saint, Betsie ten Boom. But now these words of Paul ring out loudly in my ears, in this unique and wonderfully paroxysmal time in human history. They describe well the unique time I believe we are just now beginning to enter into more fully. Jesus said,

> "I have told you these things so that in me you may have peace. In this world you will have trouble (tribulation NKJV). But take heart! I have overcome the world" John 16:33.

I believe the seals of Revelation chapter six began to be opened as early as the spring of 2010, marking the onset of a new dimension of "tribulation" outlined in the scriptures. As my husband, Dave, and I travel throughout Asia on our missionary journeys, we often see serious tribulation already taking place in areas such as Orissa, India, where so many Christians were murdered or burned alive in their homes only a few years ago.

Therefore, it's on the birth pangs of this final global tribulation, that I will take some time to look more closely at the examples of "deeper still" described in 2 Corinthians 4:7-11 by the apostle Paul. As we enter into this period that others also are describing as the beginning of tribulations, we take heed to the words of Jesus in Luke 21:26, *"Men will faint from terror, apprehensive of what is coming on the world ..."* In Luke 21:29 He says,

> *"Look at the fig tree and all the trees. When they sprout leaves, you can see for yourselves, so when you see these things happening, you know that the kingdom of God is near."*

The "fig tree" mentioned here is generally considered in many instances to represent Israel. After many years of being scattered, Israel came into being as a nation in 1948, along with a number of other nations throughout the world, the "other trees" that Jesus mentions here.[3] In verse 32 He says, "I tell you the truth, this generation will certainly not pass away until all these things have happened." The generation within which Jesus is speaking has surely passed away, but Jesus is referring to the generation who sees the "fig tree" and the "other trees" mature and sprout leaves. Having been born on May 4, only 10 days before the nation of Israel, on May 14, 1948, I consider myself to be in "this generation." As such I fully expect to see "these things" written about in Luke chapter 21, and with them the return of our Lord Jesus Christ to planet earth.

When I am speaking to groups, I sometimes make the statement that "I don't expect to die." And I speak that in all truthfulness. However, people have looked shocked as they consider that I may be claiming some supernatural powers to stay alive far beyond my expected natural years. Gradually it dawns on them that I am saying I genuinely expect to see the return of Jesus to the planet within my natural lifetime. When this soaks into their awareness a little deeper, it usually causes some challenges to the paradigms they are holding onto.

But whether I have perceived accurately or not, the majority of Christians will not deny that we are on the verge of very difficult times both in America, and throughout many countries of the world.

For this reason, I have written the book, **Deeper Still**, because it will remind us of the source of strength, endurance and comfort offered by our Lord Jesus, who has gone through tribulations on our behalf, and is prepared to gird us up through these times.

"Where can I go from your Spirit? Where can I flee from your presence? If I go up to the heavens, you are there; if I make my bed in the depths, you are there. If I rise on the wings of the dawn, if I settle on the far side of the sea, even there your hand will guide me, your right hand will hold me fast."

Psalm 139: 7-10

Chapter Two

"We Are Hard Pressed ..."

As the apostle Paul writes his second letter to the Corinthians, he is urging them to stand firm with good courage. In 2 Corinthians 4:1 he says, *"Therefore, since through God's mercy we have this ministry we do not lose heart."* And in the following verses, 7-11, he gives these admonitions:

> *"But we have this treasure in jars of clay to show that this all-surpassing power is from God and not from us.*
>
> ***We are hard pressed on every side, but not crushed; perplexed, but not in despair; persecuted, but not abandoned; struck down, but not destroyed.***
>
> *We always carry around in our body the death of Jesus, so that the life of Jesus may also be revealed in our body. For we who are alive are always being given over to death for Jesus' sake, so that His life may be revealed in our mortal body."*

As I compare my personal experiences with some of those persecutions that are currently being experienced by our affiliated ministers and missionaries in parts of Asia and Africa, I have to admit that I am actually quite short of claiming an understanding into the full depth of meaning in these verses. However, I believe they hold a key to our preparedness for the coming tribulation that is already unfolding.

Second Corinthians 4:7b states: *"... this all-surpassing **power** is from God and not from us."* **"Power,"** here in the Greek is *"dynamis,"* meaning: power, ability; miracle, or ruler.

Verse 8a says, "We are **hard pressed** on every side but not **crushed**." **"Hard pressed"** in Greek is *"thlibo"* meaning: to press upon, crowd up to, to be pressed, troubled, persecuted, or harassed. And the word **"crushed"** in Greek is *"stenochoreo"* meaning: to be crushed, or to be restricted.

Isaiah 53:5b says, *"...He was crushed for our iniquities..."* Here the word, *crushed* in Hebrew is *"daka"* meaning: to crush, to be crushed, be dejected, be humbled, or to lie crushed.

Within the Body of Christ there seems to be a common consensus that this passage of Isaiah chapter 53 refers prophetically to the suffering of Christ on the cross. We know that Jesus' bones were not literally crushed, according to John 19:33. However, His spirit was crushed with the weight of all mankind's sin for all of history – past, present and future. Though pictures of Jesus on the cross give him a loin covering, history reflects that He and the other men crucified were shamed in being crucified naked; surely this was a terribly humiliating experience.

I am one who experiences some sense of claustrophobia when in a confined space, or when limited in the freedom of movement of my limbs. So, the experience of Christ on the cross in a peculiarly unnatural position, being entirely unable to move his members is to be "restricted" to the nth degree, adding another dimension of meaning to the word "crushed."

Isaiah 53:5b contains the best application I can find for this word *"crushed,"*

"... he was crushed for our iniquities; the punishment that brought us peace was upon him, and by his wounds we are healed."

In Acts chapter 8 we find the apostle Philip directed by an angel to leave Samaria and go to the desert road leading from Jerusalem to Gaza. On his way he met a eunuch from Ethiopia who was in charge of the treasury of Candace, queen of the Ethiopians. He was coming from Jerusalem where he had gone to worship God; perhaps he was a proselyte to Judaism, or a god-fearing Gentile. God had seen and heard the Ethiopian's heartfelt offerings of worship in Jerusalem, and now God could see the Ethiopian's sincere attempts to understand this uniquely descriptive passage in Isaiah chapter 53. As the Ethiopian read the Isaiah passage, God read his heart, and God was moved by the sincere heart's cry for more insight into the meaning of this passage. So God spoke to the evangelist Philip in Samaria, and Philip was directed by the Spirit of God to go to the Ethiopian's chariot and stay near it. As Philip asked the Ethiopian if he understood what he was reading, the Ethiopian responded, "How can I, unless someone explains it to me?" He invited Philip to come up and sit with him to explain the passage to his understanding. He was reading from Isaiah 53, starting in verses 7-8:

"He was oppressed and afflicted, yet he did not open his mouth; he was led like a lamb to the slaughter, and as a sheep before her shearers is silent, so he did not open his mouth. By oppression and judgment he was taken away. And who can speak of his descendants? For he was cut off from the land of the living..."

Acts 8:35 says Philip used this Isaiah passage to explain to the Ethiopian the good news about Jesus. Isaiah 53:4-5 states:

"Surely he took up our infirmities and carried our sorrows, yet we considered him stricken by God, smitten by Him and afflicted. But he was pierced for our transgressions; **he was crushed** *for our iniquities; the punishment that brought us peace was upon him."*

These scriptures of Isaiah chapter 53 have been accepted throughout the centuries as a most poignant and descriptive picture and depiction of Jesus' sufferings on the cross on our behalf to purchase our salvation. In Acts chapter eight we see that the Ethiopian eunuch heard these things and believed in the Lord Jesus. He was baptized right there in the desert in whatever body of water Father God provided at that moment for them.

Through most of my Christian life I had accepted this passage as descriptive of Jesus' sufferings, and it had become exceedingly meaningful to me in expanding my under-standing of Jesus as the suffering Messiah.

And then one day some years ago, God opened my heart and understanding to reveal a much deeper truth within this passage. It was concerning the eunuch's "connection" in the spirit with the suffering servant, Jesus. God opened my eyes to see that verse after verse of Isaiah 53 seemed to describe the Ethiopian's own unique suffering. Verse 7b says,

"...he was led like a lamb to the slaughter, and as a sheep before her shearers is silent, so he did not open his mouth."

In the Ethiopian eunuch's life there had been an earlier day, possibly as a child of 10 or 11, when he had been sold or conscripted from his family and carried off against his will to serve in the courts of the queen. It was the practice then to make these male servants in the queen's court "safe" by castrating them. In this state they would then have no male hormones to promote a desire for sexual relations; nor would there be any ability to achieve penetration to make this possible.

I believe the Holy Spirit gave the eunuch a very special revelation when he read verse 7:

"He was oppressed and afflicted, yet he did not open his mouth; he was led like a lamb to the slaughter, and as a sheep before her shearers is silent, so he did not open his mouth."

I believe he may have seen a memory glimpse of himself as he had been led away to experience the heinous deeds that would make him a eunuch, forever depriving him of his manhood, and removing from his life any hope for a future wife or offspring.

He may have been required to endure the cutting or crushing of his testicles without being allowed even an opportunity to cry out in the incredible pain this would have produced. Perhaps he would have been threatened with death if he cried out in his agony. So, in Isaiah 53:7 the eunuch read, "He was oppressed and afflicted, yet he did not open his mouth." So perhaps even in this detail there was a point of similarity in his experience. Then in verse 8 we read:

"By oppression and judgment he was taken away, and who can speak of his descendants? For he was cut off from the land of the living..."

Here again we see a point where the eunuch may have discovered Jesus' identification with His own circumstances, being denied any future hope of any descendants.

Jesus was not similarly maimed, but He chose a life of singleness and abstinence, perhaps a great sacrifice. He could therefore identify with every normal man's battle to be sexually pure in thought and deed.

And then in verse 10 we read:

"Yet it was the Lord's will to crush him and cause him to suffer, and though the Lord makes his life a guilt offering, he will see his offspring and prolong his days, and the will of the Lord will prosper in his hand."

A great sense of awe flooded my soul the moment Holy Spirit revealed these precious spiritual secrets of how the Ethiopian eunuch could have found his own "crushing" circumstances described in the passages of scripture that foretold the future sufferings of Christ the Lamb of God.

The Ethiopian had gone to Jerusalem to seek out and worship God, though he didn't know God personally. God so saw, heard and honored the Ethiopian's quest, that He sent Philip, one of His most effective evangelists of that day, to a solitary desert place, for the sake of *one broken man* who was suffering and searching for the truth about God, the testimony of God, and the personal touch of God upon his own life.

The Ethiopian eunuch had been "crushed" in his physical body, "crushed" emotionally as future hopes were forever daunted, and "crushed" in his spirit, wondering how he could encounter a real and living God who could identify with and give meaning to his suffering.

And in one brief encounter, the Ethiopian met with a man of God who could interpret through the Spirit of God the reality of the Word of God into his life. I believe the Ethiopian eunuch saw in this Isaiah chapter 53 passage the extraordinary portrait of a God who had already been "crushed" in His sufferings. This man he read about could identify so wonderfully with the particular sufferings the Ethiopian eunuch had endured, from the day he was torn, stolen or sold from his family – to endure such an unfair and heinous mutilation and destiny.

And in these verses he discovered the Savior's identification with his own suffering. This revelation caused him to immediately believe and receive this God-man Jesus into his heart and life. God saw his heart's desire to seal the transaction for all eternity with the act of baptism, and He provided adequate water, even in the midst of a desert.

This story is one of my favorites in the entire Bible. Like the parable Jesus taught of the shepherd who left the 99 sheep to go after the one who was lost (Matthew 18:12-14), Jesus sent His servant Philip to a desert place for the sake of *one broken man* who was sincerely searching for a tangible reality in God.

Our souls wonder, "Why?" I believe the answer is two-fold. First, God cared deeply for the eunuch's sincere desire to know God in an intimate way. As Philip was explaining the meaning of the text to the eunuch, it is as though the eunuch was hearing the voice of God saying to him, "I know where you are; I know how you feel."

And, secondly, it was because He had a unique destiny in mind for the eunuch. History tells us that this one man went back to Ethiopia and shared the gospel of salvation and new life in Jesus Christ, and that entire region of the world exploded with new life. It seems the eunuch, in his physically sterile state, had become one of the most prolific evangelists of all history. And then Isaiah 53:8 opened itself even more poignantly to his understanding:

"By oppression and judgment he was taken away, and who can speak of his descendants?"

But he who had no physical descendants would have countless spiritual descendants, as life in Christ was birthed to believers and disciples in a significant portion of the world.

Like Jesus, who had no physical descendants, he now had more spiritual descendants than he could ever count. His life, once tormented with grief and confusion, now had taken on a new purpose and destiny in Christ.

Returning to our key verse in 2 Corinthians 4:8a we read: **"We are hard pressed on every side but not crushed..."** In writing these verses to the Corinthians, I believe he is saying that even the most pressing and painful circumstances we may encounter in life don't need to entirely crush us, because Jesus has already been crushed for us:

"But He was pierced for our transgressions; He was crushed for our iniquities; the punishment that brought us peace was upon Him, and by His wounds we are healed" Isaiah 53:5.

Jesus' agonies of the pre-cross beatings, the nearly impossible trek to Golgotha's hill, the unimaginable sufferings of the hours on the cross, and the unknown horrors of the grave produced a crushing that is **"deeper still"** than the current situation which Paul describes as **"hard pressed on every side, but not crushed."**

The Ethiopian eunuch's story is so very comforting and encouraging to me, in that God cared enough for the one man's longings and searching, that He met him where he was in his "desert place." And there is likewise hope for each of us in the "desert places" where we might find ourselves in the course of our lives. God knows who we are and where we are; He alone has all power to hear our prayers and even the nonverbal groaning of our hearts ... and He can answer according to His purposes for us.

We can know with certainty that He is there with us, identifying with our sufferings and helping to carry whatever "cross" we are bearing at the time.

I revisit and briefly summarize again the book, *The Hiding Place,* by Corrie ten Boom. During World War II she and her family hid Jews in their home, who were trying to escape the Nazi's program of extermination. As Nazi soldiers discovered what the family was doing, the entire family was arrested, and Corrie and her sister Betsie were forced to endure continual, horrendous sufferings in the concentration and extermination camps. Several times in the book, her sister Betsy's heartfelt and profound statement is repeated:

*"There is no pit so deep that He is not **deeper still.**"*

"He" of course, being Jesus Christ of Nazareth, her Savior and close friend.

Psalm 139:7-10 comforts and encourages our hearts in the truth that there is no place so high, nor so low that He is not present:

*"Where can I go from your Spirit? Where can I flee from your presence? If I go **up to the heavens,** you are there; if I make my bed in **the depths**, you are there. If I rise on the **wings of the dawn;** if I settle on the **far side of the sea**, even there your hand will guide me; your right hand will hold me fast."*

These four verses describe the *extremes of vertical and horizontal space.*

The psalmist's question was, "Where can I go from your Spirit?" And the proceeding verses answer the question... "Nowhere."

"Why are you downcast, O my soul? Why so disturbed within me? Put your hope in God, for I will yet praise Him, my Savior and my God."

Psalm 42:5

Chapter Three

"We Are Perplexed..."

In the verse, 2 Corinthians 4:7 Paul wrote:

> *"But we have this treasure in jars of clay to show that this all-surpassing power is from God and not from us. We are hard pressed on every side but not crushed;* **perplexed, but not in despair***; persecuted, but not abandoned; struck down, but not destroyed."*

Perplexed in Greek is "aporeo," meaning "to be puzzled, at a loss, perplexed, wondering. Perplex = to confuse, bewilder.

Despair in Greek is "exaporeo," to be in despair. The Webster's dictionary describes despair as "complete absence of hope; to abandon all purpose or hope."

We ask ourselves the question, "When did Christ experience the extreme of bewilderment to the point of being in utter despair (a "complete absence of hope") on our behalf?"

In the Garden of Gethsemane, Jesus prayed earnestly for some period of time. The manner and matter of His prayer was so heavy that He beseeched the disciples to stay awake and carry some of the weight of this prayer burden with Him:

> *"My soul is overwhelmed with sorrow to the point of death. Stay here and keep watch with me"* Matthew 26:38.

We may only assume that in this time of prayer, the Father was revealing some measure of understanding and preparation for what the next grueling events of His life would hold for Him.

But even His disciples failed Him, for when He came back to them, He found them sleeping yet again. Already in these moments of severe disappointment, the crucible of the cross had begun to press in upon Him. Even His closest friends could not stay awake to see Him through and pray with Him during what were most likely some of the most emotionally grueling and tempting moments of His life,

"For we do not have a high priest who is unable to sympathize with our weaknesses; but we have one who has been tempted in every way, just as we are – yet was without sin" Hebrews 4:15.

Jesus had worked through the temptations of Satan in the wilderness at the outset of His ministry and He came out victorious. But this was a temptation of a very different sort. I believe that in that garden the Father gave Jesus a glimpse of the sufferings He was going to experience in the coming hours. Crucifixion was a common punishment in that day, and Jesus might possibly have even seen it being inflicted upon others; though we have no record of this in the scriptures. He knew in advance that His death would be by crucifixion, in order to fulfill the prophecies about the suffering Messiah:

"'But I, when I am lifted up from the earth, will draw all men to myself.' He said this to show the kind of death He was going to die" John 12:32.

But have we ever considered that His greatest temptation may have been to walk away right then, in the garden, before the Roman guards came to arrest Him? It was not too late to at least attempt an escape from the hours of indescribable agony that He knew awaited Him. This was perhaps His greatest battle, yet His beloved ones had disappointed Him. He had only asked them to *"watch and pray"* while He prayed; yet His dear friends had forsaken Him and slept through it.

I have a photo framed on my wall next to my favorite chair, which I took in Israel some years ago. It was of a nearly life-size sculpture of Jesus praying in agony upon a great rock in one area of the Garden of Gethsemane. It just so happened that when we were there it was almost noon on a bright sunny day. One of the large olive trees was casting a shadow over Jesus' lower torso and legs, while His upper torso and arms were still in the bright sunlight.

I didn't realize at the time what a poignant image this was. But when I saw it as a finished print, I immediately recognized that I had caught "real-life" images of what I think took place in the Spirit as Jesus prayed and wept upon the rock. Even then the darkness of His hour of suffering was beginning to creep over Him, and I believe He could feel and sense it, especially while His closest friends had failed to stay awake with Him in His neediest time: "Could you men not keep watch with me for one hour?" Matthew 26:39b.

And yet ... even then He arose from the rock and faced the ones he knew would take Him to His suffering and death. Even tasting in some small measure the upcoming agony He would face, He chose not to flee from it. He won this mountainous battle over temptation on our behalf. I am reminded of the scene on the cross where the onlookers jeered at Him to come down from the cross *if He was really the Messiah.*

But He had already triumphed to some extent over the enemy in His second temptation in the wilderness at the onset of His ministry immediately after His baptism. In the Luke 4:9-11 account of it we read:

> *"The devil led Him to Jerusalem and had Him stand on the highest point of the temple. 'If you are the Son of God' he said, 'throw yourself down from here. For it is written: He will command His angels concerning you to guard you carefully; they will lift you up in their hands so that you will not strike your foot against a stone.' Jesus answered, 'It says: Do not put the Lord your God to the test.' "*

I've taken a few paragraphs to consider these moments in the garden, for they set the stage for His cross experience, where we see Jesus was *perplexed*. In Matthew 27:46 and Mark 15:34, at the 9th hour Jesus cried in a loud voice, "My God, my God, **why have you forsaken me**?" In these verses I see that Jesus seemed perplexed by the events taking place, and then His state of feeling forsaken is nothing short of despair. The Greek definition of despair is: the *"complete absence of hope"* or "to abandon all purpose or hope."

We can't read these two passages without sensing to some degree Jesus' expression of *"complete absence of hope."* Even Father God had abandoned Him in His most dark and difficult hours.

Whatever the content of the Father's revelation to Jesus at the prayer rock in Gethsemane the night of His betrayal, the revelation of it doesn't seem to have included the degree of despair Jesus would experience on the cross on our behalf. Perhaps even the unexpectedness of the Father's abandoning Him is what caused it to be so perplexing (wondering, confusing, bewildering) to Him – leading up to and including complete "despair."

We must seek to somehow comprehend that Jesus was utterly forsaken in order that we wouldn't need to be utterly forsaken. He had experienced the extreme for us, so we could endure everything in between the emotional state of being "perplexed" and that of being "in despair," by His grace at work within us. Hebrews 13:5 says, *"Never will I leave you; never will I forsake you,"* quoting God's declaration to Joshua before Joshua took over the leadership of Israel.

And Jesus said in Matthew 28:20b, *"And surely, I am with you **always**, to the very end of the age."* The word "always" in Greek is "hemera" meaning "day, time of the day, indefinite period of time, day after day, every day."

If we combine these definitions into one, it could read like this:

"Surely, I am with each and every one of those who are mine, every day, all day, for all time."

So, as we conclude our study of "perplexed but not in despair," these following truths somewhat summarize our discoveries:

Jesus embraced the complete abandonment and absence of hope for us, in order that we might always have hope – *not* given over to despair. Even when we are perplexed, as the circumstances and events of our lives don't seem to make sense or have a reason, we can still have hope and not despair. He endured despair so we could have hope.

His life and the power of His Spirit within us give us hope in the midst of our difficult circumstances that can seem overwhelming, needless or without reason.

His victory over sin and death give us the hope of eternal life with Him, no matter what we face or suffer in this life.

His Word gives us some understanding into His ultimate purposes for us. As we read Romans 8:28 we see that *"all things work for the good of those who love Him, who are called according to His purposes."* And even when we can't clearly see His revealed purposes, verse 29 gives us the ultimate purpose, that we might be conformed into His image by the things we experience, and the trials we suffer:

"For those God foreknew He also predestined to be conformed to the likeness of His son, that He might be the firstborn among many brothers" Romans 8:29.

As I looked for an example of some "real people" who exemplified in their lives a state of being perplexed but not in despair, again my thoughts turned to Corrie ten Boom and her sister Betsie, who were abducted with their father from their watch and clock repair shop in Holland, transported like animals, and placed in horrific concentration camps in Germany during the reign of the Nazis in World War II. Their courageous story described how they endured the terrible persecution of these months and years – from solitary confinement to near starvation, to freezing temperatures, to beatings, to excruciatingly heavy work requirements, to lice and flea infested, overcrowded circumstances, to the death of their father and friends, and to the ever-present fear of death by lethal gas any day. Yet in all this, they did not despair, because they had a purpose; they had a hope and they had His presence.

The first purpose was one that pleased the Lord greatly, I believe. As Jewish people were being sought out by the Nazis, imprisoned and exterminated, the Ten Boom family worked with the "underground" to help move these people to safe places where they would not be discovered. The family fearlessly held to this purpose, loving and caring for those dear to the Father's heart, even though they knew they may eventually be discovered and incarcerated.

Once they were discovered and imprisoned, their purpose was to serve and encourage others, while leading as many as possible to faith in the Lord Jesus Christ.

In her book, Corrie comments on how much more loving and purposeful was Betsie's attitude than her own. On one occasion while they were in the prison camp, they were moved to an overcrowded lice-infected sleeping area. Corrie was appalled and discouraged to some degree; while Betsie immediately commented on the advantages of it, since the Nazi guards would not come into the infested area, and Corrie and Betsie would be able to share the message of Jesus with more ease to more people. Throughout this indescribably awful time, they were upheld by the awareness of Jesus' presence, and by their strong convictions of the purposes He had for them in that place.

In the decades since the Nazi holocaust, political leaders, students of history and ordinary people have continued to be perplexed by the progression of the Nazi terrorism to the degree of depravity it reached – and yet leaders and governments were slow to take action to set things right and stand up against such demonic tyranny.

But in spite of it, there were those like Corrie and Betsie who found peace and hope in the presence of the Holy Spirit and the scripture's promises of eternal life through their faith in Jesus Christ. He experienced the ultimate despair to purchase for us that hope.

"We have this hope as an anchor for the soul, firm and secure. It enters the inner sanctuary behind the curtain, where Jesus, who went before us, has entered on our behalf. He has become a high priest forever, in the order of Melchizedek" Hebrews 6:19-20.

"But let all who take refuge in you be glad; let them ever sing for joy. Spread your protection over them, that those who love your name may rejoice in you. For surely, O Lord, you bless the righteous; you surround them with your favor as with a shield."

Psalm 5:11-12

Chapter Four

"We Are Persecuted..."

Going back to 2 Corinthians chapter four, we read in verses 7-9:

*"We are hard pressed on every side, but not crushed; perplexed, but not in despair; **persecuted, but not abandoned**; struck down, but not destroyed."*

Although my husband, Dave and I have led a Christian mission organization since 1994, this word "persecution" took on new meaning for us a few years ago. We had corresponded with a missionary in Orissa, India for several years, since he had attended a leadership seminar we taught in Bangalore, India in 1997.

Then suddenly near Christmas time, 2008, a sudden cry came to us from Pastor T. via email. Hindu radicals by the hundreds were on a rampage through parts of Orissa state. Dozens of people were murdered on the streets or burned alive in their homes as Molotov cocktails were tossed inside by the terrorists. The brutality continued on for days as they systematically sought out and murdered Christians. The more fortunate fled into the nearby jungles to save their lives. There was no clean water there and very few edible plants, so many were in serious condition when it was finally somewhat safe to return to their villages. Our friend Pastor T. had hidden in an upper room of his compound for days until the rampage was over. Thankfully the radicals didn't discover and slaughter the orphans who were in their care in the back portion of their property. The photos passed on by email from Pastor T. were difficult to look at – so many burned-out homes of village pastors, some with the charred bodies of burned family members still visible among the rubbish. Our hearts were melted in almost unbelief and sympathy – so many pastors and/or wives and children had been lost, and of those who had survived, their houses had been destroyed.

We rallied a siege of prayer on their behalf and set about raising money to help them begin to bury their dead and rebuild their homes. By God's grace thousands of dollars passed through our hands to assist in the rebuilding, and soon pictures of their rebuilt homes began to come to us from Pastor T.

"Persecuted" had never come so close to home for us before.

Voice of the Martyrs, a Christian mission magazine, and other publications covered these events, and the Christian world was awakened to this monumental eruption of persecution.

We in America have been somewhat isolated from this degree of persecution. That is, until the Twin Towers in New York City imploded before our eyes on our TV screens about ten years ago. A new age had begun for America – an age that ended naïve and childlike attitudes concerning the condition of the world, for some. It was a sobering time that redefined *security* for most, and a time that awakened Americans to a new definition of the word "persecution."

Most American Christians are fairly isolated from the realities of this word, "persecution" and it's implications in our lives. We have had a difficult time envisioning real persecution in America.

But it has begun and will rapidly escalate in this coming decade in America. A number of people we know already have "safe places" prepared for persons fleeing persecutions – both Christians and Jews. I believe we all need to prepare our hearts and minds to see Matthew chapter 24 begin to unfold before our eyes in this generation in America, even as Christians and Jews in the middle-east and Asia have experienced it for decades.

But 2 Corinthians 4:9 says we will be *"persecuted but not abandoned."* Webster's definition of "abandoned" is "to forsake, leave, abandon, desert, give up completely."

The words abandon or abandoned bring to mind a search for a child who has wandered away from a campsite, or a mountain climber who never came down from the mountain. Usually all kinds of search efforts are exhausted, including search dogs, helicopters, and all available means for a number of days. Then if the missing person is not discovered, a pronouncement is finally made that the "search has been abandoned." When we hear this on the news broadcast, our spirits sort of fall, even if we didn't know the person ourselves. For without a continued search, all hope is gone; the inevitable must be reckoned with ... lost without hope.

But 2 Corinthians 4:9 says we are "persecuted but not abandoned." And again scripture reveals that because He was abandoned, we don't have to be. Jesus experienced in His flesh and spirit the extremes of these most negative states, in order to spare us from experiencing them, or to enable us to find His presence and peace within them.

Let us briefly consider Matthew 27:46 and Mark 15:34, which quote Jesus as saying in Aramaic (a language commonly spoken in Palestine at that time) *"Eloi, Eloi, lama sabachthani?" "My God, my God, why have you forsaken me?"*

The note in my Bible next to this passage points me to the introduction to Psalm 22, verses 1-2. Here we can almost hear the heart of Jesus saying,

> *"My God, my God, why have you forsaken me? Why are you so far from saving me, so far from the words of my groaning? O my God, I cry out...but you do not answer..."*

Then in Psalm 22:19 there follows a prophetic description of Jesus' suffering on the cross:

> *"But you O Lord, be not far off; O my strength, come quickly to help me."*

Psalm 22 is commonly accepted as representative of the Lord's passion on the cross, and Jesus quotes Psalm 22:1 in Matthew 27:46 and Mark 15:34.

These three references indicate that Jesus was expressing His sense of complete abandonment by the Father during His most intense moments on the cross. Second Corinthians 5:21 says,

*"God made Him who had no sin **to be sin** for us, so that in Him we might become the righteousness of God."*

I have heard it taught that as He carried such a burden of sin for the entire span of the history of the world – past, present and future, He actually *became* sin, and the presence of the Father and the Holy Spirit had to lift off of Him.

We can conclude that Jesus experienced the sense of being entirely abandoned on our behalf. And even though we may be abandoned by some of our earthly kin and acquaintances, God will not abandon us. Interestingly in Psalm 16:9b-10 David says,

"... my body also will rest secure, because you will not abandon me to the grave, nor will you let your Holy One see decay."

My Bible's text note states that these verses are ultimately fulfilled in Christ, and indeed the Father did rescue Jesus from the grave unto eternal life.

Matthew 27:46 says, *"My God, my God, why have you forsaken me?"* Interestingly, as I studied these words *"forsaken"* and *"abandoned,"* I pondered if there could be a difference between the two words. I came to the conclusion that it is possible for one to be forsaken but not abandoned. This hit me as a sad reality in the lives of so many. This week one of our sons and his wife were, in a court hearing, awarded full custody of two young daughters of another relative. The girls were literally almost abandoned by their single mother as she went to jail for drug manufacturing and using. But long before their abandonment, they had been forsaken in their experiences of deprivation, neglect and cruelty. Thankfully their circumstance was seen by God, and He powerfully undertook for them. Never before have I seen such a dramatic example of Proverbs 21:1:

> *"The king's heart is in the hand of the Lord; He directs it like a watercourse wherever He pleases."*

The judge in this case was so entirely moved by the history and record of their repeated abuse and neglect, that he executed judgment swiftly to place them in a safe and loving family on a permanent basis. They are now "at home" in their new home, enjoying their lovely, clean, decorated lavender room ... already, in faith, prepared for them even before the judge's decision had been made. It is a living example of Jesus' love and care for us, as Jesus says:

> *"I am going there to prepare a place for you. And if I go and prepare a place for you, I will come back and take you to be with me that you also may be where I am"* John 14:2b-3.

But regardless of how we define or categorize these things, our Savior has experienced them, and paid the price to suffer them on our behalf. As Betsy Ten Boom would say to her sister

Corrie, *"We must tell people what we have learned here. We must tell them that there is no pit so deep that He is not deeper still. They will listen to us, Corrie, because we have been here."* And though Betsy soon found her final solace in the Savior's arms there within the prison's makeshift hospital, Corrie did indeed tell their story for literally millions to read over the past four decades, and it will surely continue to echo throughout the years to come. Perhaps no other book (except the Bible) has touched the lives of so many to bring comfort amidst their unique experiences of persecution of one sort or another. I believe it has encouraged myriads of people to look a little more hopefully into His Word, listen a little more intensely for His voice, and hold on a little more tightly to His admonition, *"I will never leave you nor forsake you"* Joshua 1:5. We can do likewise, experiencing His presence by the Spirit, even when our flesh cries out that we seem abandoned.

"The Lord is my shepherd ... He leads me beside quiet waters, He restores my soul. He guides me in paths of righteousness for His name's sake. Even though I walk through the valley of the shadow of death, I will fear no evil, for you are with me..."
Psalm 23:1-4a

Chapter Five

"We Are Struck Down ..."

Looking again to Second Corinthians, we read in verses 4:8-9:

> *"We are hard pressed on every side, but not crushed; perplexed, but not in despair; persecuted, but not abandoned;* **struck down, but not destroyed."**

In studying "destroy," I happened upon Jesus' words in John 17:12, speaking of His twelve disciples:

> *"While I was with them, I protected them and kept them safe by that name you gave me. None has been lost except the one doomed to destruction, so that Scripture would be fulfilled."*

This *destruction* reserved for Judas Iscariot is the ultimate place of *destruction* designed for the wicked who have totally rejected God. Another *destruction* verse here is worthy of our investigation, because it leads us on a treasure hunt of discovery seemingly experienced by very few to date.

We must investigate Psalm 88. This Psalm is attributed to the writings of the sons of Korah, the Levitical choir made up of the descendants of Korah appointed by David to serve in the temple. A leader in the days of David was Heman, to whom the writing of this Psalm is credited.

I have read Psalm 88 in a number of translations and searched the study notes extensively. All the references at my disposal attribute to Psalm 88 something similar to the note in my Zondervan NIV translation which reads, "A cry out of the depths, the edge of death, whose whole life has been lived, as it were, in the near vicinity of the grave. So troubled have been his years that he seems to have known only the back of God's hand, God's wrath."

At this point I want us to read Psalm 88 anew, asking Holy Spirit to enlighten our understanding to revelation perhaps not generally understood by the Body of Christ. Psalm 88:1-18 says:

"O Lord, the God who saves me, day and night I cry out before you. May my prayer come before you; turn your ear to my cry. For my soul is full of trouble and my life draws near the grave.

I am counted among those who go down to the pit. I am like a man without strength. I am set apart with the dead; like the slain who lie in the grave, whom you remember no more, who are cut off from your care.

<u>You have put me in the lowest pit, in the darkest depths</u>. Your wrath lies heavily upon me; you have overwhelmed me with all your waves. You have taken from me my closest friends and have made me repulsive to them. <u>I am confined and cannot escape</u>; my eyes are dim with grief. I call to you, O Lord, every day; I spread out my hands to you.

Do you show your wonders to the dead? Do those who are dead rise up and praise you? Is your love declared in the grave, your faithfulness in Destruction? Are your wonders known in the place of darkness, or your righteous deeds in the land of oblivion?

But I cry to you for help, O Lord; in the morning my prayer comes before you. Why, O Lord do you reject me and hide your face from me? From my youth I have been afflicted and close to death; I have suffered your terrors and am in despair. Your wrath has swept over me; your terrors have destroyed me. All day long they surround me like a flood; they have completely engulfed me. You have taken my companions and loved ones from me; the darkness is my closest friend."

I believe that in these verses the psalmist is actually prophetically describing a part of the "grave experience" of our Lord, in a similar way to that in which Psalm 22 describes some aspects of the "cross experiences" of Jesus.

Second Corinthians 5:21 says:

*"God made Him who had no sin to **be sin** for us, so that in Him we might become the righteousness of God* (New International Version).

So often it seems we see Jesus as speaking His final words, "It is finished," on the cross, and interpret them as meaning that the entire work of purchasing our redemption was accomplished on the cross. But how could this be, since many others had suffered similar deaths, even more lengthy or painful ones than Jesus did on the cross? The two men who surrounded Jesus on their crosses had their legs broken, perhaps representing more pain than what Jesus experienced.

I would like to propose that Jesus' declaration "it is finished" had quite a different meaning for His life and our life in Him. The scripture says that *"He was tempted in every way as we are, yet was without sin,"* Hebrews 4:15. Sometimes I think we grossly under-estimate the incredibly challenging assignment and accomplishment it was for the God-man Jesus to fulfill this requirement for a complete and utter absence of sin in His life.

As He struggled in the garden before His arrest He said, *"My soul is overwhelmed with sorrow to the point of death"* Mark 14:34. Then in verse 36 He asks, *"Take this cup from me. Yet not what I will, but what you will."* He did not sin even once against the holy requirements of Father God, even in His heaviest assignment, and I believe *"It is finished"* is akin to the phrase, *"I did it!"* which a runner might exclaim at the end of a long and exhausting marathon race.

I believe in this statement Jesus is referring to having lived His entire life within a human body, resisting all the temptations common to man, and in this last exclamation, the work of living the sinless life was finished. He did it! He made it to the finish line without sin. He met all of the Father's righteous requirements. *He had become the perfect and sinless sacrifice for our sins.* What a feat! And how fitting was His exclamation, *"It is finished."*

But no, I do not believe His entire work to secure our salvation was finished, because His was no ordinary death. He took upon Himself all the sins of all mankind for all the years of history. Hebrews 7:27 states, "He sacrificed for their sins *once for all* when He offered Himself." He had actually *become sin* for us, and as such He was destined for judgment and destruction. John 17:12b quotes Jesus as saying of Judas, *"None has been lost except the one doomed to destruction so that Scripture would be fulfilled."*

The sufferings I quoted from Psalm 88 may be a prophetic representation of His suffering in the grave and in Hell itself. And because He carried the sins of all men for all time (including those of Judas) He was destined for destruction even as Judas was.

Luke said in Luke 12:5,

"But I will show you whom you should fear. Fear Him who, after the killing of the body, has power to throw you into hell."

We have been engaged in lengthy and arduous arguments with some who say that Jesus didn't go to hell. But I would argue, "Why would He *not* go to hell, if He was wearing the sins of all mankind placed upon Him on the cross?" If His suffering on the cross was no more arduous than those men previously crucified, how could He have suffered for the sins of all men for all time? No, I believe Jesus "did His time" in the place of death and destruction until the just penalty of every sin of every human of every day for all time was fulfilled (including those sins of future generations yet unborn).

Another testimony is the Apostles Creed, which has been quoted by millions throughout Church history, and continues to be a foundation stone of faith for countless believers and congregations.

"I believe in God the Father, Almighty, Maker of heaven and earth, and in Jesus Christ His only begotten Son, our Lord; who was conceived by the Holy Ghost, born of the virgin Mary; suffered under Pontius Pilate; was crucified dead and buried. <u>He descended into hell. The third day He rose again from the dead.</u> He ascended into heaven, and sits at the right hand of God the Father Almighty. From thence He shall come to judge the quick and the dead. I believe in the Holy Ghost. I believe in the holy catholic church, the communion of saints, the forgiveness of sins, the resurrection of the body, and the life everlasting. Amen."

Another point to consider is found in Ephesians 4: 7-10:

"But to each one of us grace has been given as Christ apportioned it. This is why it says: 'When he ascended on high, he led captives in his train and gave gifts to men.' (What does 'he ascended' mean except that <u>He also descended to the lower, earthly regions?</u> He who descended is the very one who ascended higher than all the heavens,

in order to fill the whole universe)."

Then Ephesians 1:19-23 reveals the power that triumphed over death and destruction.

"That power is like the working of His mighty strength which He exerted in Christ when He raised Him from the dead and seated Him at His right hand in the heavenly realms, far above all rule and authority, power and dominion, and every title that can be given, not only in the present age, but also in the one to come. And God placed all things under His feet and appointed Him to be head over everything for the Church, which is His body, the fullness of Him who fills everything in every way."

Destruction and death are swallowed up in victory. Hebrews 7:15 states regarding Jesus,

"And what we have said is even more clear if another priest like Melchizedek appears, one who has become a priest not on the basis of a regulation as to His ancestry, but on the basis of **the power of an indestructible life."**

We may be struck down by our circumstances, or even by death. But because Jesus conquered even death and its terrors and was seated in the heavenlies, so shall we be seated with Him – until that soon-coming day when He returns with the saints in heaven to reign upon the earth for 1000 years. I can't help but think of the countless men and woman who have trusted in the Lord Jesus Christ as

Savior and Lord, and yet they have been struck down – and even perished – by an accident, a terrible storm, a fatal illness, an act of war, a murderer, some other fatality, or even martyrdom. We are indeed very saddened when we learn of these things, and we can't help but wonder at the *why* of them. Some things we may never understand until we can discuss them in the presence of Jesus ... and perhaps then it won't matter, because we'll see those who were struck down, in their place at Jesus' side in their glorified bodies.

Herein lies our hope and promise. Though we may be struck down and humiliated by our circumstances, or may even taste death, if we have trusted in Jesus as our Lord and Savior, we will be "***like Him, for we shall see Him as He is***" 1 John 3:2b. *And He is our High Priest "on the basis of the power of an indestructible life"* Hebrews 7:16b. So shall we, who have trusted in Jesus Christ for salvation and known Him as Lord, have an indestructible life for all ages with Him. We thank God that though at times we may be struck down – as we trust in Him we are not destroyed.

"He was despised and rejected by men, a man of sorrows, and familiar with suffering ... He was despised, and we esteemed him not. Surely he took up our infirmities and carried our sorrows."

Isaiah 53: 3-4a

Chapter Six

Jesus Is Deeper Still

In this chapter I want to return again to the last words of Betsie ten Boom before she was taken to the hospital within the concentration camp, where she soon passed to be with the Lord:

> *"...must tell people what we have learned here. We must tell them that **there is no pit so deep that He is not deeper still**. They will listen to us, Corrie, because we have been here."*

I want to provide us with a "faith base for grace" upon which we can truly build a fortress of faith to prepare and protect us in difficult days ahead, no matter what we may be facing in our lives. From one who suffered more tribulation than most of us can even imagine, came words that will echo through the darkest days and years of the past and the current generations, and the remaining generations until Jesus Christ's return to earth. I want to amplify what meaning I have gleaned from Betsie's most profound statements, and provide for us a skeleton of scriptures that build a strong foundation of faith for these challenging years to come. We can refer back to this "faith base for grace" when times are difficult, or when we tend to be discouraged by the events of life unfolding in our midst unexpectedly, discouragingly and sometimes overwhelmingly.

The first of these truths is that "God is deeper still." I believe Betsie is saying that no matter how low she has found herself in the lice and flea infested, overcrowded, disease-laden, forced labor and torture-driven, sleep-deprived, degrading, humiliating and indescribably horrible position ... Jesus had been there for her and with her. He had been one step ahead of her in each unfolding layer of inhumane and horrifying depravity.

I am reminded of Psalm 22 and Psalm 88, which prophetically describe portions of Christ's sufferings on the cross and after the cross. I can acknowledge that Jesus suffered the penalties of sin for all people for all time and was in the place of "deepest depths" for us all ... even the depths of hell itself. *"There is no pit so deep that He is not deeper still"* proves true especially in this understanding, if we can grasp it. And if we can fathom it, Psalm 22 prophetically describes portions of Christ's sufferings on the cross. Psalm 88 goes on at least *four times* deeper into the indescribably horrific place of the "darkest depths" in a *confinement He could not escape,* that place called *"Destruction"* (8b,11).

Jesus asks in Psalm 88:11, "Is your love declared in the grave, your faithfulness in Destruction?" I consulted the Zondervan NIV Concordance for the meaning of this word "Destruction" with a capital "D" found in Psalm 88: "The Hebrew word for destruction is 'baddon' meaning 'destruction ... the Place of Destruction (the realm of the dead).'"

But even though I can grasp the concept of Jesus going into hell to suffer the due punishment for sin, what about the required suffering for all kinds of sickness and diseases?

Isaiah Chapter 53 is prophetically written about Jesus and describes this truth so wonderfully. A few verses come to mind:

> *"He was despised and rejected by men, a man of sorrows, and familiar with suffering ... surely He **took up our infirmities and carried our sorrows**, yet we considered Him stricken by God, smitten by Him and afflicted. But He was pierced for our transgressions, He was crushed for our iniquities; the punishment that brought us peace was upon Him, and by His wounds we are healed"* (v. 3-5).

Matthew affirms the healing power of Jesus' sufferings in Matthew 8:14-17:

> *"When Jesus came into Peter's house, He saw Peter's mother-in-law lying in bed with a fever. He touched her hand and the fever left her, and she got up and began to wait on Him. When evening came, many who were demon-possessed were brought to Him, and He drove out the spirits with a word and healed all the sick. This was to fulfill what was spoken through the prophet Isaiah: 'He took up our infirmities and carried our diseases'"* Isaiah 53:4.

In considering these lofty verses, I am reminded of a phrase my mother used on occasion, "The proof is in the pudding." I'm not sure what the pudding proved, except perhaps that the cooker was a good cook. But we generally take it to mean that the proof of a paradigm or theory is how it is played out in real world, real time, real event occurrences. So I feel compelled to share what I believe to be one of the most profound experiences with the Holy Spirit that I can remember in my 60+year lifetime.

Let me however first preface this account by sharing with you the condition of our worship experience in the years Dave and I had been married. I had been blessed with a good musical sense of tone and scale. I had played saxophone in Jr. High and High School and had sung in choirs and small groups over the years. But in Dave's history, he had been hesitant to sing anywhere. He played guitar, but even then, he had great difficulty in tuning his own guitar, and would often turn it over to another to help him with tuning, because he had almost no sense of pitch or tune. We loved to worship together, but it was somewhat challenging at times, for he "couldn't carry a tune in a bucket" so to speak.

Then things changed. One of my most dramatic spiritual experiences happened when Dave and I had gone to the college town where our daughter and son-in-law were studying. On the five-hour drive across Washington State, we had started to compose the words to a new song, and had struggled together as we searched for musical notes to match the composed verse.

While we were there in the college town, we went to the Sunday service at the church near campus where they had been attending. It was a very large church, and the worship had been quite stirring to my heart. The pastor then began to preach on Isaiah 53, verse by verse. In retrospect, it seems to me that he was focusing heavily on the healing power of Jesus, as described there so wonderfully. Suddenly the power of the spirit overwhelmed me, and I began to weep uncontrollably. My daughter was on one side of me, and Dave on the other. They wondered what had overtaken me but didn't want to interfere with what the Lord was doing, so they didn't disturb me. Dave held my hand as I wept on and on in my seat for what seemed to be a long time. I could not control my sobbing; nor could I truly understand what was happening in my soul.

I struggle to define it, but I had felt an overwhelming grief over my sin, that had caused Jesus so much pain and agony in these verses of the "suffering servant" found in Isaiah chapter 53. It was as if the sins I would sin NOW would somehow continue or lengthen the amount of suffering He was experiencing on the cross BACK THEN, though this paradigm didn't make much logical sense. I remember grieving deeply over my sin, and pleading with many tears to God that He would help me overcome my sin and sinful nature. I felt intense remorse that my sin had caused Him so much pain and grief, and I didn't want to grieve Jesus even more with current and future sin. Now there was no grossly obvious sin such as immorality, murder and the like ... but rather the day-to-day failures of ordinary life.

Dave held my hand and tried to comfort me with his presence next to me. Finally, after what seemed like many minutes, I regained my composure; the service ended and we went home. In our kids' tiny apartment Dave picked up our son-in-law's guitar and began to play something. Suddenly he yelled out from the bedroom where he was sitting, "He's healed my voice! He's healed my voice!" I ran in to behold and listen to him singing *in tune* to the worship songs we so often had struggled through. I added, "He has also healed your ears so that you can detect the right note and then match your voice to it." I can't describe the tremendous joy we experienced that day as we began to sing and worship together "in tune" for the first time in our years of marriage. The thrill of it was beyond description.

As the amazement subsided, we tried to discern what had happened. We finally realized that the tremendous anointing I had experienced in the worship service (defining for me in a new way the purchases of the Suffering Servant, our Lord Jesus, described in Isaiah chapter 53) had brought about the healing of my beloved as he held my hand in empathy and support of the profound spiritual experience I had been having. This was my first, and one of the most dramatic and wonderful, of the many healings I would see firsthand in my years of experience as a missionary.

And returning to consider one model in the faith, Betsie ten Boom, these verses found in Isaiah chapter 53 are only a few of the verses prophetically describing the suffering of our Lord Jesus on Betsie's behalf. And the story answers in part the question, *"Who can speak of His descendants?"* Though Jesus had no wife or physical descendants, He has had innumerable descendants, among them the humble and brave Betsie ten Boom, who saw Him as "deeper still" beneath her almost unbearable situations; and able to lift her up under the most painful, weighty and horrible circumstances. And heaven will reveal the tidal wave of souls who were swept into the kingdom of Heaven amidst the horrific circumstances of those prison camps she and Corrie found themselves in. Corrie and Betsie's lives and the message of the Savior they brought to hurting women there in their imprisonment, birthed a new generation of saints – descendants of the King of Kings.

"Out of the depths I cry to you, O Lord; O Lord, hear my voice. Let your ears be attentive to my cry for mercy... I wait for the Lord, my soul waits, and in His word I put my hope. My soul waits for the Lord more than watchmen wait for the morning, more than watchmen wait for the morning."

Psalm 130:1-2, 5-6

Chapter Seven

God Is With Us

Another priceless truth to remember is that **"God is there with us, no matter what our circumstances."**

A key passage is **Psalm 69**, starting with *verse 1:*

> *"Save me, O God, for the waters have come up to my neck. I sink in the miry depths, where there is no foothold. I have come into the **deep** waters; the floods engulf me... Rescue me from the mire; do not let me sink; deliver me from those who hate me, from the **deep** waters. Do not let the floodwaters engulf me, or the **depths** swallow me up or the pit close its mouth over me ... They gave me vinegar for my thirst ... I am in pain and distress; may your salvation, O God, protect me. The Lord hears the needy and does not despise His captive people."*

Here David describes poignantly the deep trouble he was in, even prophetically touching Christ's experience on the cross. Yet a little later in Psalm 71 we can read some of his prayers written in his old age; so God had been faithful to stay with him, bear him up under his earlier circumstances, and give him strength to *"declare Your power to the next generation, Your might to all who are to come"* Psalm 71:18. We are a part of the *generations* who are greatly encouraged by the privilege of reading these stories and psalms of God's faithfulness towards him in all of the "deep pits" of his life.

For another example, I love to look at the words of Isaiah 7:10-14. The Lord has sent prophets to King Ahaz in a time of great fear and unrest. Verse 10 reads, *"Again the Lord spoke to Ahaz. 'Ask the Lord your God for a sign, whether in the <u>deepest depths</u> or in the <u>highest heights</u>.'"* Here God Himself declares that He is capable of giving to Ahaz a sign, "whether in the **deepest depths** or in the **highest heights**." These regions are owned and controlled by the almighty God whom we know and serve, and He is perfectly able to be there in the places that are "deeper still" than those positions we are currently experiencing. The sign God gave him (Isaiah 7:14) was one we now treasure – the sign of the virgin who would give birth to a son, who would be called Immanuel.

We could also read Psalm 139 to remind ourselves of God's omniscience, omnipotence, and omnipresence (He knows, has control over, and dwells within every circumstance.)

The most descriptive verses in our current *quest are verses 7-10.*

"Where can I go from Your Spirit? Where can I flee from Your presence? If I go up to the heavens, You are there; if I make my bed in the depths, You are there. If I rise on the wings of the dawn, if I settle on the far side of the sea, even there Your hand will guide me; Your right hand will hold me fast."

Surely, in every place we can imagine, He is indeed "deeper still."

The Lord's words to Joshua are also very encouraging: "As I was with Moses, so I will be with you; I will never leave you nor forsake you. Be strong and courageous..." Joshua 1:5-6. The words of Jesus in Matthew 28:20b however, are perhaps even more convincing and comforting: *"And surely I am with you always to the very end of the age."* God is indeed with us; here I believe the promise is until and into the millennium, when He will return to reign in the flesh.

In considering some current "real life; real time" testimonies, I remembered the mining accident in Copiapo, Chili about a year ago. On August 5, 2010 a mine cave-in trapped 33 miners 700 meters (2300 feet, or almost ½ mile) below the ground in the 121-year-old copper-gold mine. Seventeen days after the accident, one of eight boreholes drilled by the rescue operators hit the precious target, and a note taped to the returning drill bit read (in Spanish) "We are well in the shelter, the 33." What a thrill to learn the miners were alive!

So, after 69 days trapped deep underground, on October 13, all 33 men were brought safely to the surface, one at a time through a narrow cylinder, over a period of almost 24 hours. I will quote part of the testimony preserved in "WIKIPEDIA, August 2010 Copiapo Mining Accident" regarding the 33 miners' experience during their 69-day entrapment deep underground:

*"Miners asked for religious items such as Bibles and crucifixes. The men set up a makeshift chapel in the mine, and Mario Gomez, the eldest miner, spiritually counseled his companions and led daily prayers. Among the miners, a number attributed religious significance to events. The wife of the first man rescued noted, 'We are really religious, both my husband and I, so **God was always present**. It is a miracle; this rescue was so difficult; it's a grand miracle.'"*

Both government representatives and the Chilean public have repeatedly credited "Divine Providence" with keeping the miners alive, while the Chilean public viewed their subsequent rescue as a miracle. Chili's president, Sebastian Pinera stated, "When the first miner emerges safe and sound, I hope all the bells of all the churches of Chile ring out forcefully with joy and hope. Faith has moved mountains..." When Esteban Rojas stepped out of the rescue capsule, he immediately knelt on the ground with his hands together in prayer, then raised his arms above him in adoration."[4]

This Wikipedia source describes a portion of the scope of the rescue plan, at the outset of the mine emergency:

"Once the government rescuers knew that the men were alive, Chile implemented a comprehensive plan to both nurture the workers during their entrapment and to rescue

*the miners **from the depths**. It included deployment of three large, international drilling rig teams, nearly every government ministry, **the expertise of the United States' NASA space agency** and more than a dozen multi-national corporations."*

Tears came to my eyes as I read this portion of the report and realized that expertise from some of the **highest heights** had been implemented to assist with this rescue of thirty-three men from some of the **lowest depths** experienced by man in real time on planet earth!

The first paragraph of this testimony stands as a good summary of a major reason, if not the most important reason, that all the 33 men survived the 69-day ordeal in a living room-sized space nearly ½ mile below the earth's surface. The wife of a miner testified:

*"...**God was always present**. It is a miracle; this rescue was so difficult, it's a grand miracle."*

"...He also descended to the lower, earthly regions ... He who descended is the very one who ascended higher than all the heavens, in order to fill the whole universe."

Ephesians 4:9-10

Chapter Eight

Only Jesus Was Forsaken

"My God, my God, why have you forsaken me?" Psalm 22:1.

> *"From the sixth hour until the ninth hour darkness came over all the land. About the ninth hour Jesus cried out in a loud voice, 'Eloi, Eloi, lama sabachthani?' which means, 'My God, my God, why have you forsaken me?'"* Matthew 27:45-46.

Luke's account of Jesus' last living moments bears consideration also:

> *"It was now about the sixth hour, and darkness came over the whole land until the ninth hour, for the sun stopped shining. And the curtain of the temple was torn in two. Jesus called out with a loud voice, "Father, into your hands I commit my spirit." When He had said this, He breathed His last"* Luke 23:44-46.

The concepts Luke packs into these two verses are so profound, I believe we could search them out for hours. Here, Father God directed a scene so visual that none could miss seeing it, and He moved the writers of scripture to record it for us, so we could see it also more than two millennia later.

This narrative takes my imagination back to a recent video I watched, which contained various options one could investigate either before or after viewing the main feature. The index of the film presented several options, such as interviews with the main characters, brief stories "behind the scenes" in the making of the movie, and other interesting or *dramatic aspects* of producing the film.

In a similar *"theatrical"* fashion, we see Father God was "setting the stage" in an unmistakable drama that illustrated to all who were present at the crucifixion, and all future readers of the scriptures over the many subsequent centuries ... the truth of the Father's literal and virtual abandonment of Jesus upon the cross. *A thick darkness covered the sun,* and for three hours God's "back was turned" so to speak from Jesus' presence. These last words of Jesus as recorded in the gospel of Matthew, "My God, My God, why have you forsaken me?" describe the truth of His condition. Father God had indeed forsaken Him, abandoning Him in His deepest moments of suffering on the cross, and handing Him over to the accompanying terrors of the next three days: the darkness of death, the aloneness of the grave, and for those who believe it, the punishments in hell itself.

We see how Luke packed into these three small verses, (Luke 23:44-46) several of the major themes of our faith. The first is the point we just looked at, that is: **Jesus was truly forsaken and abandoned by God the Father.** It was not an image, but a reality. Second Corinthians 5:21 says that He *became sin* for us. If you have ever seen a piece of petrified wood, you can visualize more fully this paradigm. Over time and pressure, the tiny particles of wood have been replaced one by one by the components of stone, so that the piece still appears to be wood, but has indeed become a piece of pure stone. On the cross the perfect holiness of our Savior was replaced, sin upon sin for all the people of the world for all time past and all time future, so that He literally *became sin* for us. Second Corinthians 5:21 says, *"God made Him who had no sin to **be sin** for us,* so that in Him we might become the righteousness of God."

I believe the deepest place man has ever been is underneath the sins of the entire world for all of time. And yet in this place Jesus never lost sight of the Father. Amidst the darkness Jesus cried out, *"My God, my God, why have you forsaken me?"* Though He experienced being forsaken by the Father, He doesn't lose His identification with the Father as "My God."

And **nevertheless, He was able to commit himself into the hands of the Father.** He cried out ... *"Father, into your hands I commit my spirit"* (Luke 23:46b). This is another major theme of our faith. And when we experience the places of deepest "darkness" in our lives, the grace of Jesus is there to aid us as we commit ourselves into the hands of the Father. Jesus has been to that deepest place of suffering and abandonment, in order that we need not ever be truly abandoned by God. For God has said in Hebrews 13:5b-6:

"Never will I leave you; never will I forsake you. So we can say with confidence, 'The Lord is my helper; I will not be afraid. What can man do to Me?'"

And within Luke 23:45 we see another major brick for the structure of our faith: *"And the curtain of the temple was torn in two."* **The need for the priest to offer the Old Testament sacrifices for sin behind the veil of the temple was ended**.

*"Day after day every priest stands and performs his religious duties; again and again he offers the same sacrifices, which can never take away sins. **But when this priest had offered for all time one sacrifice for sins,** He sat down at the right hand of God. Since that time He waits for His enemies to be made His footstool, because by one sacrifice He (Jesus) has made perfect forever those who are being made holy"* Hebrews 10:11-14.

This is a cornerstone passage for the foundation of our faith, but so often we see it forgotten or omitted from the faith testimony of so many believers. For instance, consider the awesome movie that showed a few years ago, "The Passion of the Christ." I personally know a number of people who believed and received Jesus as their Lord and Savior during or as a result of this very vivid and passionate expression of the life and death of our Savior, Jesus Christ. However, like so many depictions of the work of Christ, it doesn't quite give us the full story of His redemptive work on our behalf.

For Jesus fulfilled in every way the sacrificial system set up in the Jewish faith. The above verse in Hebrews describes the work of Jesus, in ascending into heaven and offering His own bloody body upon the altar in heaven, once and for all completing the sacrifice for the sins of all people for all time. On that first Resurrection Day, He completed the most dramatic and effective journey from the lowest of the lowest places, to the ultimate highest place at the right hand of the Father in Heaven, completely fulfilling the requirements of the Jewish sacrificial system, and purchasing "once for all" our redemption from sin and death. To stop at the cross is not enough; to worship at the empty tomb is insufficient. We must look further ... to the altar in Heaven, where Jesus went to the highest place to complete in every measure the fullness of the system of the law.

Another testimony in Ephesians 4:9-10 says:

"...He also *descended to the lower,*
earthly regions ...He who descended is the very one who ascended **higher than all the heavens** *in order to fill the whole universe.*"

Here we can see perhaps the ultimate *deeper, higher* expression in the scriptures. And Hebrews 12:2 states:

"*Let us fix our eyes on Jesus, the author and perfecter of our faith, who for the joy set before Him endured the cross, scorning its shame, and sat down at the right hand of the throne of God. Consider Him who endured such opposition from sinful men, so that you will not grow weary and lose heart."*

As we consider Jesus' choices, what will we do? Is our Father worthy to be trusted? Even in a sense of deepest abandonment, Jesus is able to trust the Father with His spirit ... all that He has left. He has carried every sorrow, every anxiety, every illness (Isaiah 53:4-5), and with the last molecule of living matter and energy He had left–even in those very last moments, He committed Himself to God the Father.

Thankfully for us, even in this the *deepest* darkest place of Jesus' life, there was a grace to trust the Father. This grace is available to us. Who is willing to fellowship His sufferings in this way? The issue is our desire, our willingness, or our grace to abandon ourselves into the Father's hands ... even as Jesus did in His place of deepest pain and abandonment (Luke 23:46a). We can truly trust in the work of this naked man on the cross, who has born all of our sins, sorrows, disappointments, pain, loneliness and abandonment.

Recently I was immeasurably blessed and enlightened as I sat for two days under the teachings and life testimony of Reverend Setan Aaron Lee. This modern saint was a medical student in Cambodia when the Khmer Rouge took over the country and initiated their "reign of terror and murder." I will quote several paragraphs from his book, where he describes events that took place following terrible sufferings as their prisoner, including being buried alive up to his neck for two days and nights in an area plentiful with poisonous snakes and wild animals. He had watched many of his friends tortured by the guards, having acid poured on their faces, eyes gouged out, and other heinous forms of torture. Then here is his personal testimony of experiencing the true God:

"Countless times I considered ending it all by committing suicide as many of my friends had done. However, something in me told me to keep going – I would make it through all of this."

Just as he convinced himself that he could make it, the unthinkable thing happened. His student ID card which he had hidden in a small pocket in his pants was found! The ID card told his captors that he was a member of the educated class, a city dweller, and an arch enemy of the Khmer Rouge. He was immediately sentenced to die along with four other students.

They were bound, blindfolded, and led to an open field. Setan stood helplessly and heard the cries of his friends as they were hacked to death with a bamboo branch that had no leaves, just deadly sharp barbs. He felt the spatter of the warm blood of his friends on his face as each one died an agonizing death. He was the only one left – now it was his turn to die. Setan began to cry out, *'Lord of the Universe, whoever you are, please spare my life!'*

Where had those words come from? Never in his Buddhist upbringing had he ever prayed a prayer like that. His executioners shoved him to his knees and he felt the bamboo branch that had killed his friends close to his neck, ready to fall and send him to his death. Setan felt sure this was his end. There was no escape.

As Setan Lee waited for the deadly blow, a loud voice screamed from behind him. 'Stop! We must investigate this man further?' What?! There was no such thing as investigations in the killing fields. And, there was never an investigation prior to an execution! Setan's mind was racing with these thoughts, not having any idea what would happen next.

The blindfold was yanked from his eyes and they immediately fell on the ghastly scene of the mutilated bodies of his fellow students. He instantly knew that whomever or whatever he had screamed out to just moments before had spared his life. He knew in his heart that he had just left his Buddhist upbringing to now serve this new found faith – whatever it was." [5]

Then the Khmer Rouge put him to work to design an irrigation system to bolster the faltering rice production of the nation. Though he was still a prisoner, he was rescued from the immediate presence of "the killing fields."

Some time later he was able to escape into Thailand, evading the numerous mines in the minefields by treading on the dead bodies of those who had not been able to avoid the deadly mines. After several days and nights in this eerie jungle, he encountered a strange man, dressed very poorly and seeming barely alive. He was scared to death by this man who jumped out toward him. Then the man asked him, "Do you believe in the Lord of the Universe?" When he was too stunned to answer, the man repeated to him again, "Do you believe in the Lord of the Universe?" Then he remembered that he had prayed to "the Lord of the Universe" when he had been nearly killed by the guards of the Khmer Rouge. To quote his book again:

"Setan looked into his eyes and exclaimed, 'Yes. I do believe in the Lord of the Universe.' 'His name is Jesus Christ,' the man said to Setan. 'Would you like to accept Jesus as your Savior and Lord? He will give you eternal life. You and I may not have much time. Any minute now, either of us could step on a land mine and die!' Setan answered, 'Yes, I accept Jesus as my Savior!' Then almost as quickly as he had appeared, the tattered prophet disappeared into the jungle as gunfire flew over their heads."

After more than a month in these minefields, he was able to cross the Cambodian-Thailand border into safety. And in the months and years to come, his life has not been directed toward the study and practice of medicine, as it was before the Khmer Rouge captured him. God had a much broader destiny waiting for him. Instead, his life has been devoted to travelling around the world to numerous cities in every continent declaring the love and generous salvation of the "Lord of the Universe, Jesus Christ of Nazareth." You can read more of his experience in the book I have quoted: *Miracles In The Forgotten Land and Beyond* by Setan and Randa Lee of Transform Asia ministries, with Shelba Hammond by Xulon Press, 2010.

Just why did I feel the unction to share this portion of Rev. Setan Lee's miraculous testimony with you? Certainly, in my six decades of life, I have never encountered any experience quite as "deep" as those I have included in these brief sections of his text. For me, they give new meaning to the phrase, "deeper still." These experiences and others he relates in his book, are almost more than one can stand to read, nor even begin to ponder. Yet we see how in the midst of them, when there was no way of escape from imminent death, the Lord of the Universe gave him the grace to call out for his life to be spared. And in this unfathomably "***deep***" place, Jesus Christ, the Lord of the Universe showed Himself to be "***deeper still.***" Even in this God-forsaken land and government, Jesus was the one who heard Setan's heart cry to a god he believed would hear him, though Setan didn't know his name. The one true "Lord of the Universe" heard his cry and delivered him out of an impossible situation. God delivered him into a life of meaning and purpose, more fruitful for the kingdom of God than he could ever have imagined. These impressions from Rev. Setan Lee rank right alongside those we gain from Corrie and Betsie Ten Boom who coined the statement, *"There is no pit so deep, that He is not deeper still."*

I pray that He will reveal Himself to you likewise to be "deeper still" than the deepest places of doubt, fear, lack or suffering you may be experiencing at this time.

"Those who cling to worthless idols forfeit the grace that could be theirs. But I, with a song of **thanksgiving***, will sacrifice to you. What I have vowed I will make good. Salvation comes from the Lord. And the Lord commanded the fish, and it vomited Jonah onto dry land."*

Jonah 2:8-9

Chapter Nine

Praise Precedes Deliverance

About 20 years ago I experienced a season in my Christian walk that was perhaps more transforming to my life and spirit than any previous season, with the exception of the day I asked Jesus to be my Lord and Savior. I want to share this with you before our exploration together is finished.

I had been asked by the elders of our church to chair a committee to prepare for a mini-conference that was to be held there about six months later. The speaker was Jack Taylor, and the conference centered around his book, *Hallelujah Factor*.[6] So the first thing I did was purchase the book and I began to read it. Little did I know it would be one of the most profound and life-changing experiences of my Christian life.

I remember stuffing the new book into my carry-on bag before a trip I was making from Seattle to Kansas City to visit relatives. There, settled in the plane with my soda and a package of peanuts I began to investigate this intriguing book. Soon I knew that Mr. Taylor was really on to something, and several hours later upon landing, I said to myself, "I'll never be the same again." I knew in my gut that the precepts presented in that book would change me, but I couldn't have guessed that it would transform my lukewarm Christian walk into a roaring fire –

truly a greatly renewed faith walk with God. I wish I could relate every principle to you, but there is one that stands out in my mind after all these years. And that is the concept that "praise precedes deliverance." Let's look briefly at a few specific scriptural examples.

Jonah's Story: We see in chapter one that Jonah had run away from God's assignment for him to preach to the wicked city of Nineveh, calling the people to repentance. A great storm came up, and the boat he was in had nearly capsized. The men finally threw Jonah overboard, sensing strongly that his disobedience to God was the root cause of their trouble. The story tells us in Jonah 1:17: "But the Lord provided a great fish to swallow Jonah, and Jonah was inside the fish three days and three nights."

In chapter two, verses 1-6 Jonah recounts his experience and emotions as he sank "into the deep, into the very heart of the seas." And within his dark "deep belly" experience he undergoes an attitude adjustment just in time:

"When my life was ebbing away, I remembered you, Lord, and my prayer rose to you, to your holy temple. 'Those who cling to worthless idols forfeit the grace that could be theirs. **But I, with a song of thanksgiving, will sacrifice to you.** *What I have vowed I will make good. Salvation comes from the Lord.' And the Lord commanded the fish, and it vomited Jonah onto dry land"* Jonah 2:7-10.

Here we see a glimpse of the "attitude adjustment" God achieved in Jonah during his "deep belly experience." God brought a correction to Jonah's reluctant and judgmental attitude toward Nineveh, and toward his assignment from God to go there to preach to the people; in other words, Jonah let go of his "worthless idol" attitude and mind set (Jonah 2:8). This resulted in an exchange of his stubborn and disobedient attitude, for one of thanksgiving before God. His change of heart and his act of thanksgiving resulted in his delivery, as the whale vomited him out onto dry land.

I wonder how many times I've been like Jonah – disregarding God's clear directions to me, and going my own way – then expecting God to bless me anyway. In times like these it's good to look for and deal with any "worthless idol" object, attitude or experience that may be standing in the way of blessings God has for us. We can ask the Holy Spirit to produce in us a thankful heart, trusting that *"... in all things God works for the good of those who love Him, who have been called according to His purpose"* Romans 8:28. Next let's look at Psalm 50:14-15:

"Sacrifice thank offerings to God, fulfill your vows to the Most High, and call upon me in the day of trouble; I will deliver you and you will honor me."

Many of us can think of times in our lives when giving thanks in a difficult situation is truly a sacrifice. Our natural minds want to dwell on the problem or lack we may be experiencing. We begin to feel sorry for ourselves, and our *pity-party* gets to rolling over our attitude, taking us deeper into a place of sadness, hopelessness, and sometimes even an attitude of resentment or anger towards God.

Notice that verse 23 says, *"He who sacrifices thank offerings honors me..."* The obvious implication here is that to give God thanks amidst difficult situations is truly a *sacrifice*. It involves giving up our unthankful, grudging, or resentful attitude (Jonah's "worthless idol"), and looking for anything and everything we can give thanks for. Thanksgiving and praise are keys to releasing God's additional resources and anointing into our lives.

This has been a poignant exercise for me personally during these weeks of recovery since my head injury and concussion ... not only the ugly 38 stitches in four different areas of my face, and the resulting infections requiring three rounds of antibiotics. But the remaining scars, persistent dizziness, and short-term memory loss have also been extremely challenging in light of my natural tendencies to be "on top of things" and keep pressing with my usual routine and my "to do list."

One day in frustration I just sat down and turned on the TV. Low and behold, there was a documentary of sorts that dealt with sports-related head injuries. And there before my eyes marched images and stories of numerous men and women (mostly young) who had suffered head injuries from various sports-related activities. Many were wheel-chair bound, and most had lost control of at least some part of their bodies' functions. Some facial expressions were distorted; some arms or legs had impaired function; and some people had impaired mental capacity that severely challenged their ability to go on with their studies. The program highlighted the attitude or inner strength of each one that empowered them to go on with their lives, graduating from high school, or fulfilling other goals they personally had set for themselves.

Right then and there I heard a *"CRACK"* in the spirit, as the Great Physician took ahold of me and made a necessary *attitude adjustment.* Holy Spirit helped me repent of my "down in the mulligrubs" attitude, and He turned my attention to all the things I had to be thankful for. My injuries were far less severe than most of those I saw on TV; and yet the ones I watched were triumphing over their circumstances. I saw a clip of one young man in a wheel-chair (football head injury) going forward to receive his High School Diploma; and other similar stories moved my heart in the direction of a right attitude towards my own less severe circumstances.

I recall my experience a few weeks ago when in the lobby after the church service, a friend commented on something that had happened only a few days earlier. I stopped and searched my memory for a moment but found nothing. Finally, I said to her rather jokingly, "Sorry, I can't seem to find any memories from that time; please tell me about it." She paused for a moment and then filled me in on the events I could not remember, and we discussed her take on them.

So, I'm learning gradually how to let others graciously "fill in the memory gaps" for me in this season. It's still too early to know if this is a temporary condition or not, but I am purposing to give God a sacrifice of praise for all the healing He has already brought to me, and for sparing me from even worse consequences of such a severe accident.

I have found it helpful in times like these to revisit and remember Biblical examples of the principle that "praise precedes deliverance." Acts 16:22-34 tells the story of Paul and Silas, who were being accused in verses 20-21 of *"throwing our city into an uproar by advocating customs unlawful for us Romans to accept or practice."* Verses 22-26 tell us more:

> *"The crowd joined in the attack against Paul and Silas, and the magistrates ordered them to be stripped and beaten. After they had been severely flogged, they were thrown into prison, and the jailer was commanded to guard them carefully. Upon receiving such orders, he put them in the inner cell and fastened their feet in the stocks. About midnight Paul and Silas were praying and singing hymns to God, and the other prisoners were listening to them. Suddenly there was such a violent earthquake that the foundations of the prison were shaken. At once all the prison doors few open, and everybody's chains came loose."*

Here we see clearly the paradigm that "praise precedes deliverance." And as I have typed this last paragraph, my heart sensed anew a second principle that is worth mentioning:

My praise may produce not only my own deliverance; but it may also assist in or precipitate the deliverance of others in a similar experience.

We might take a moment to ponder how our experience of praise and thanksgiving may have helped to bring someone else with a similar circumstance into a change of heart or attitude, that frees them to be and do all that God has intended for them in His divine plan.

Interestingly, just this week I was introduced to the friend of a friend of mine. While our common friend was in surgery, we got to know each other better, as we conversed in the hospital waiting room.

Janice (interestingly the same age with the same first name) had a stroke a few years ago, and though she has recovered from the subsequent paralysis, she still suffers with short term memory loss. We have exchanged a number of stories related to this little handicap, and both of us have found comfort in simply being "understood" clearly by another human being. She even remarked on how it has helped her attitude as she has had opportunity to share stories and commiserate with someone who understands something of this life challenge. What an awesome Papa God we have who could surprisingly delight the hearts of His "little girls!"

"Sacrifice thank offerings to God, fulfill your vows to the Most High, and call upon me in the day of trouble; I will deliver you, and you will honor me."

Psalm 50:14-15

Chapter Ten

Offering Thanksgiving

Truly "praise" and "thanksgiving" are such close first cousins that they look a lot alike – so much alike that it's sometimes hard to tell them apart. So before we leave their neighborhood, let's take a look at some related concepts that may enlighten us:

"Not only so, but we also rejoice in our sufferings, because we know that suffering produces perseverance; perseverance (produces) character; and character (produces) hope" Romans 5:3-4.

The Bible says, *"...we also rejoice in our sufferings, because we know..."* – but do we really *know* the above things to be true? And are these qualities attributes that we even desire in our lives? Perhaps in our *Microwave TV Dinner* society we don't value perseverance, character and hope very much in our lives; we quickly try to flee sufferings, not stopping to consider that there could possibly be a built-in result, or even a reward at the other end. It seems we so often tend to make everyone around us miserable with our complaining, moaning and groaning in the midst of them. And for most of us it is very challenging, if not impossible to get a glimpse of the rainbow on the other side of the rainstorm. But in this life, we *will* have difficulties, heartaches and sufferings – the question is not *if* we will have them. Shortly before His betrayal and arrest, Jesus said to His disciples, *"In this world you will have trouble (tribulations). But take heart! I have overcome the world. John 16:33b."* His firm past-tense declaration of victory has always caused me to ponder a little, for the agonies of betrayal, beatings and the cross were still awaiting Him. But the Father had revealed at least some of these events to Him in advance, and He had even spoken of them to His disciples. Yet He went forward.

"Let us fix our eyes on Jesus, the author and perfecter of our faith, who for the joy set before Him endured the cross, scorning its shame, and sat down at the right hand of the throne of God. Consider Him who endured such opposition from sinful men, so that you will not grow weary and lose heart," Hebrews 12:2-3.

There is never a question of "if" there will be difficulties, heartaches, sufferings or loss in our lives; these things will plaque each of us while we live in this world. The question is, "What will I do with what I have? Am I willing to allow the adverse circumstances to be used by God to bring honor and glory to His name, through my life?" Will I give thanks in all things, knowing that *"this is the will of God for me in Christ Jesus"* 1 Thessalonians 5:18? Or will I murmur, complain and bicker with God over my lot in life? The choice is ours. We can choose to believe the Bible and obey what it clearly declares, or we can choose to be miserable. I will quote again the verse, Romans 8:28 where Paul says,

"And we know that in all things God works for the good of those who love Him, who have been called according to His purpose."

This has been one of my favorite verses for many years. I have reminded myself of it in the midst of difficult or unpleasant circumstances, and quoted it to others who were going through some sorts of trials. But I think it took some years before I realized I had only half of the equation. The real pearl of this teaching is in the next verse:

"For those God foreknew He also predestined to be conformed to the likeness of His Son, that He might be the firstborn among many brothers" v. 29.

Here we see a clearer picture behind the difficult times in our lives. The Father wants us to be shaped like infinitely precious diamonds into the likeness of His son, Jesus. But what even is the purpose in that? There are several, but one seems to stand out above the others in my thinking.

The Father wants the world to behold His son and desire Him. *"He is patient with you, not wanting anyone to perish, but everyone to come to repentance"* 2 Peter 3:9b. And Romans 5:3 reminds us that, *"suffering produces perseverance; perseverance, character; and character, hope."*

I once visited a diamond factory and watched as the skilled workers chipped away at the crude stone to produce one facet and then another. The more facets or sides that were produced, the more radiant the diamond would become, reflecting more of the light that was available in the room. It seems that perseverance, character and hope, as seen in our lives, are like those facets focusing more of the light of Christ in our lives to be seen and desired by others. The ability to "keep on keeping on," in the presence of trials or suffering, and to do it with a cheerful heart ... can be a beautiful thing that causes others to wonder where these character strengths come from. Then we should be ready to share about the hope that we have in Christ.

"In your hearts set apart Christ as Lord. Always be prepared to give an answer to everyone who asks you to give the reason for the hope that you have. But do this with gentleness and respect, keeping a clear conscience ..." 1 Peter 3:15-16a.

Before going on we should take a closer look at the character quality of perseverance.

Perseverance may be defined as: *the ability to endure and to stand; the capacity to continue on; to carry on in the face of difficulty or opposition; or the ability to "push on through to the other side."*

Is that something you want in your life?
Consider the "Kansas Bean Story."

The Kansas Bean Story

Years ago, I was visiting Mom and Dad on their farm in Kansas, and when I would visit it was always my habit to go with Dad to look at the various animals and crops on the farm. I had loved growing up there, and through I currently was living in the city, it fulfilled the desires of some of the "farm girl" in my blood to check out these things, and it seemed to make Dad happy that I was interested.

Rain was always an issue, for it was often sporadic, and it sometimes threatened the quality and quantity of grain that we would be able to sell or use to feed the livestock. It was almost always an issue in mid to late summer, when we were looking for the crops to produce well. As for me and my two older sisters, our main concern was whether or not we would have the monetary resources on hand to go on vacation. We lived near Kansas City, and vacation was usually spent in the Rocky Mountains of Colorado. This 500+ mile drive represented a significant expenditure for the gasoline required by our trusty station-wagon, that didn't get the best gas mileage. So when it didn't rain on time and the crops were beginning to need a drink, Dad would often jokingly say, "Well, we may not be able to go on vacation." To this day I'm not really sure whether he was joking or not, but we kids started praying for rain, and somehow we never missed a year of going on vacation in Colorado. It was a highlight time of the year for us, and I'm so thankful Mom and Dad made a way for it.

Then coming to visit as an adult one year, it seemed the beans looked unusually green and robust. I mentioned to Dad that it looked like there would be a good crop. I thought he would almost automatically agree with me, but he frowned and said, "Well it remains to be seen whether they will turn out or not. This season of rains has been a little too good." I guess Dad could see the confusion on my face, and he started to explain what he meant.

"You see Jannie, it's a helpful thing if the beans and corn have some weeks when it doesn't rain, because then they are forced to put down longer and stronger roots to pull up the water from deeper in the ground. But when we get rain on a steady basis, they never have to put down deep roots. Then when we have weeks with no rain they quickly wither, because they don't have a strong enough root system to pull up the water that's further beneath the surface."

~

This explanation made perfect sense to me, and I have never forgotten the story of the beans. It has made me ponder if the same principle could be applied to our Christian lives. If we get what we need (or *think* we need) right when we need it, we come to expect it that way. So when we hit an obstacle in life's path, or a season of "drought" we sometimes tend to get dismayed, and begin to complain, murmur, or perhaps wonder if there's something wrong with our walk with God or our prayer life. Maybe we even begin to blame God for His lack of provision.

But if we have learned to experience seasons of "drought" or "lack," it teaches us a number of good lessons. We begin to realize, "Life's not just a bowl of cherries!" And we learn ways of coping that help us get through the difficult times, or seasons when it seems we have a lack of some sort. So we begin to experience that *"...suffering produces perseverance; perseverance, character; and character, hope"* Romans 5:4. Especially in these approaching *"end times,"* perseverance, character and hope are highly valued commodities for the Christian life. It is God's desire that we would offer thanksgiving while we persevere in trials and sufferings, though it is not the normal reaction of most people. But, if we will allow the Holy Spirit to instruct us, there will be several areas of notable growth in our lives. Offering praise and thanksgiving in times of trial and suffering can result in a display of God's sustaining power in the midst of our difficulties, or in the process of our deliverance. This display or testimony of our faith and trust in God glorifies Him, and results in drawing others to Jesus.

"I waited patiently for the Lord; He turned to me and heard my cry. He lifted me out of the slimy pit, out of the mud and mire; He set my feet on a rock and gave me a firm place to stand. He put a new song in my mouth, a hymn of praise to our God. Many will see and fear and put their trust in the Lord" Psalm 40: 1-3.

When we are able to offer thanksgiving and praise to our God while we persevere in the midst of trials and suffering, it will result in a testimony about our Lord which glorifies Him. It magnifies His abilities to keep and sustain us and says to others, "I can trust that ...

- God cares about what I go through."
- God loves me and is in control of my life."
- God is able to sustain me or deliver me."
- God can be trusted with your life too."

On the other hand, our murmuring, complaining or grumbling in the midst of trials or suffering, (or at any time) may result in God's displeasure and the possibility of consequences. 1 Corinthians 10:10 says, *"And do not grumble, as some of them did and were killed by the destroying angel."*

Or our negative attitude and actions can in essence provide a testimony of slander against God's character and motives towards us. In the midst of their exodus from Egypt, the Israelite community grumbled, saying, *"... you have brought us out into this desert to starve this entire assembly"* Exodus 16:3. When we grumble and complain in the midst of trials and suffering, the testimony may say:

- "God is not able to sustain me and/or deliver me."
- "God doesn't know what I am going through and He doesn't care.
- "God doesn't really love me and isn't in control of my life."
- "God can't be trusted with your life either."

Our patterns of grumbling when we are in the midst of trials and sufferings can bring a slander against God's character, love, power, authority, wisdom, compassion and other fine attributes of our Savior, Lord and King. It can result in bringing shame to His name and to the whole family of God.

But let's turn our thoughts to consider one other *positive* result. Offering thanksgiving while we persevere in trials and suffering will result in the development of God's character into our character:

> *"And we know that all things work together for the good of those who love the Lord and are called according to His purposes ... to be conformed to the image of His Son ..."* Romans 8:28-29.

> *"Consider it pure joy, my brothers, whenever you face trials of many kinds, because you know that the testing of your faith develops perseverance. Perseverance must finish its work so that you may be mature and complete, not lacking anything"* James 1:2-4.

In the Western Church today, many believers have totally lost the concept of the "prosperity of suffering" revealed in James 1:2-4. In our rejection of any form of difficulty, discipline, hardship or suffering we have scorned one of the Holy Spirit's primary *"tools"* in the maturing and strengthening process of the believer. It is possible that often, when we accuse the devil for the difficulties in our lives, we may be stealing from God the honor that could be His through the process of our perseverance in and through those circumstances. True Christian maturity includes the element of being able to *"give thanks in all circumstances"* because you know, *"... this is God's will for you in Christ Jesus"* 1 Thessalonians 5:18. This attitude brings glory to God rather than to the devil.

Increasing in God's character produces hope and spiritual fruitfulness in and through our lives.

> *"For this very reason, make every effort to add to your faith goodness; and to goodness, knowledge ... self-control ... perseverance ... godliness ... brotherly kindness ... love. For if you possess these qualities in increasing measure, they will keep you from being ineffective and unproductive (barren) in your knowledge of our Lord Jesus Christ"* 2 Peter 1:5-8.

Offering thanksgiving while we persevere in the midst of trials and suffering will result in a strengthening of our hope and faith in God to:

▪ Sustain us in and/or deliver us out of our circumstances, both now and in the future.

▪ Increase the faith of others to trust in and rely upon Him, especially during life's trying circumstances.

In Psalm 77:7-10 the writer is in distress and very cast down:

> *"Will the Lord reject forever? Will He never show His favor again? Has His unfailing love vanished forever? Has His promise failed for all time? Has God forgotten to be merciful? Has He in anger withheld His compassion?"*

But in verses 11-12 he states,

"I will remember the deeds of the Lord ... I will meditate on all your works and consider all your mighty deeds."

In verses 13-15 we see that remembering God's powerful acts has increased his faith:

"Your ways, O God, are holy. What god is so great as our God? You are the God who performs miracles; you display your power among the peoples. With your mighty arm you redeemed your people."

It is interesting to discover how in this passage we see the progression of the psalmist in his attitude and actions – from being full of doubts and very cast down in spirit – to remembering *God's powerful acts* – to recounting *God's attributes and actions:* His holiness, power, loving concern, kindness, and benevolent acts.

This shows us a very essential aspect of this process; that is, we want to progress to a point of not simply offering a *sacrifice of thanksgiving* amidst our trials and suffering. But this should move us to a position of *praising God for who He really is,* in attributes such as kindness, love, concern, strength, compassion and power. When we remind ourselves of God's attributes and begin to praise them, we come to conclusions such as: "I can rely on You because your Word is true." "I can trust You because you have proven yourself to be faithful in ALL ways. You are strong, loving, powerful, caring, and faithful." I am reminded of Psalm 42:5:

"Why are you downcast, O my soul? Why so disturbed within me? Put your hope in God, for I will yet praise Him, my Savior and my God."

In summary, **thanksgiving** amidst the situation leads us to considering and **praising God's mighty deeds** for us; and this leads us to recognizing and **praising God's attributes** of righteousness, holiness, faithfulness, truth, kindness, love ... and the list could go on and on.

We see this common progression developing in many situations found in the Bible, and also in our own experiences. We can learn to apply this progression in our own lives, in order to move forward from a position of doubt, fear and complaining ... to a place of recognizing anew God's attributes that can supersede the circumstances and bring hope.

We actually often come to a place of abandonment, in which we experience a deeper sense of peace and trust amidst our circumstances, and an attitude of willingness to surrender in a deeper way to whatever God is doing in our lives or the lives of others around us, whether we understand it or not.

*"**Deep calls to deep** in the roar of your waterfalls; all your ways and breakers have swept over me. By day the Lord directs His love; at night His song is with me – a prayer to the God of my life. I say to God my Rock, 'Why must I go about mourning, oppressed by the enemy?' ... Why are you downcast, O my soul? Why so disturbed within me? Put your hope in God, for **I will yet praise Him**, my Savior and my God"* Psalm 42:7-9, 11.

"I will" is a key phrase, because praise is initiated by an act of the will, when the emotions want to reside in (and even sometimes wallow in) the place of discouragement, doubt and even despair. This entire Psalm is well worthy of our reading and meditation. It seems as though the "spirit man" inside the psalmist is admonishing the soul of the man (his thoughts, attitudes, emotions) to wake up from their downward spiral and look up; for in the process of praising Him the soul is reminded of His mighty attributes. In this place hope arises as heart attitudes change.

*"Hear me when I call, O God of my righteousness; thou hast **enlarged me** when I was in distress; have mercy upon me, and hear my prayer"* Psalm 4:1 KJV.

"Deep calls to deep." When we have committed our lives to the Lord Jesus Christ, He resides in our spirit; His spirit is *"deeper still"* within us than the thoughts and attitudes of our minds and emotions. In that place of discouragement and questioning, we can take the advice of the Spirit to *"Put your hope in God, for I will yet praise Him."* Our change of heart and attitude can be just the medicinal spoonful of hope that can help to lift others from their place of doubt and fear – to a place of trust and faith in Jesus.

"He put a new song in my mouth, a hymn of praise to God. Many will see and fear and put their trust in the Lord." Psalm 40:3

"Let us fix our eyes on Jesus, the author and perfecter of our faith, who for the joy set before Him endured the cross, scorning its shame, and sat down at the right hand of the throne of God. Consider Him who endured such opposition from sinful men, so that you will not grow weary and lose heart."

Hebrews 12:2-3

Chapter Eleven

Purpose In The Pain

There seems to be some value in asking the Holy Spirit to help us discover the purpose in the pain we are going through, whether it is physical pain, emotional discouragement or torment, financial struggles and hardships, relational misunderstandings, separation from loved ones or friends ... or some other source of discomfort or suffering.

It is a natural and common tendency within our times of loss, pain, disappointment or suffering to wonder the "why" of it. Sometimes we have a tendency to chastise ourselves and feel guilty because we can't just accept our circumstances without wondering the "why" of them. But I believe a very normal and even useful part of the process is to dialogue with the Holy Spirit along the way to discern if possible, even if only in some small measure of understanding – the "why" of it, or at the very least some potential positive result that could come from it. Some small period of appraisal is acceptable, appropriate, and even advisable for us to consider. If we don't allow God to help us discern or define some purpose in our pain, the enemy of our souls will do it for us with accusations like: "It's all your fault; you always screw everything up; see what you've done now!" "You wondered if you could trust God to help you _____, and look what happened when you did." "Now that you've messed that up, you'll never get another chance like it again." "You knew this wouldn't work out." "You can't do anything right, and you'll never amount to anything."

Usually these suggestions and accusations are not accurate, and the intention of the enemy is to lead us to discouragement and/or despair in order to paralyze us from forward progress and the testimony for God that can result on *the other side* of the negative circumstances, or even within them. If we "camp on" these negative appraisals, they can tend to destroy our faith and hope in God. Or often, even well-meaning people will make their own appraisals of our situations. And though they may mean well, their judgments sometimes do not line up with the true heart of God for us amidst our circumstances.

I am reminded of the story in Jeremiah 29:11-14a, where we find God's people in exile in Babylon due to their disobedience. But even in the middle of this discouraging situation, the Lord brings consolation and comfort to them with His promise:

> *"For I know the plans I have for you,"* *declares the Lord, "plans to prosper you and not to harm you, plans to give you hope and a future. Then you will call upon me and come and pray to me, and I will listen to you. You will seek me and find me when you seek me with all your heart. I will be found by you," declares the Lord, "and I will bring you back from captivity."*

Sometimes our story is similar, in that our poor choices or our disobedience has led us into our place of misfortune or discomfort, and the enemy wants to separate us from God by continuing to remind us of our failures. But this awesome passage reveals God's loving-kindness, forgiveness, and ongoing purposes for His beloved people, even though their disobedience had resulted in their exile. We are His dearly loved children, and His steadfast love, mercy and forgiveness are extended to us as we acknowledge and confess our error or sin. And when our "time-out standing in the corner" is over, there is a renewed experience of His plan for our lives as we go forward with Him.

We are reminded by the Apostle Paul of one other aspect or purpose in the pain.

*"I consider that our present sufferings are not worth comparing with the **glory** that will be revealed in us"* Romans 8:18.

This glory includes the....

*"light of the knowledge of the **glory** of God in the face of Christ"* 2 Corinthians 4:6b.

And the glory is further defined in this passage as we consider that....

"We always carry around in our body the death of Jesus, so that the life of Jesus may also be revealed in our body. For we who are alive are always being given over to death for Jesus sake, so that His life may be revealed in our mortal body" v. 10-11.

"... we do not lose heart... our light and momentary *troubles are achieving for us an eternal **glory** that far outweighs them all."* 2 Corinthians 4:16-17.

When I think of the word *glory*, my mind goes back a few years to the autumn time of year in Kansas. One of the couples in the Church fellowship we attended owned and operated a Christmas tree farm. There would inevitably be a few trees that would turn brown due to old age or disease. These would need to be cut down, removed from the stand of healthy trees, and stacked in a pile apart from them.

But in the fall as it began to get cold in the evenings, the couple would always host a cook-out at their farm, inviting all the folks in the fellowship and other guests. A long table was placed in their yard for the "Pot Blessing" supper items to be displayed and consumed while it was still light. And then Keith, the owner of the property, would make a huge bonfire, using the dead wood from the trees that were cut down due to disease or death. In my memory the fire pit was about ten feet across, and the height of the fire at least 5-6 feet tall. Never before had I experienced such an awesome bonfire! As the fire blazed some of us would begin to roast marshmallows, while others would start to sing worship songs and choruses as we watched and warmed ourselves around the blaze. It was a body and heart-warming experience for all of us who were a part of that Church body, and also those who were invited guests – both believers and non-believers whom we hoped would be attracted to the warmth of fellowship in Jesus Christ that we enjoyed.

The "glory" of the huge bonfire was possible only because some trees had fallen short of their original intents and purposes – gracing the living rooms as some families' Christmas trees. But nevertheless, the inner glory of their substance was revealed magnificently as each was ignited along with others of like destiny.

It seems to me that our lives are like that so often. Things don't always work out the way we had planned. The "purpose in life" that we worked towards for years doesn't come to pass the way we had expected due to accident, illness, misfortune, loss of income, family issues, unfortunate work experiences ... and the list could go on and on. We might say we feel like the trees that never make it to the glory of the high point at Christmas in the living room.

It is at times like these that we must remind ourselves of the verses I have listed on page 113. Our triumph over the innate obstacles and disappointments of life in the power and character of the Lord Jesus Christ is intended in part for the *display of His glory and character* within us. The world needs to see a concrete display of His mighty power at work within us, helping us triumph within or over the trials that are common to life on the earth ... in order for them to desire the Author of Life, His presence, His power, and His promise of an eternal life that doesn't contain the sickness, pain or sufferings of this present world.

In these verses we see that the light of His glory is revealed outwardly; it is manifest in our lives, and it points to a future glory that will never fade away. Like the Christmas trees that didn't make it to their originally expected destiny, their life energy and essence were extravagantly displayed just in time to warm and illuminate a great fire – a fire that birthed for some who were present, watching, and listening " a new hope for life abundant and a life eternal in Him. It was an awesome display of the glory of our Creator who designed trees for many purposes; among those, to be wood that would burn with such dynamic light and warmth!

Before I leave this subject, I also am reminded that some of our lives' challenges, struggles and sufferings are designed to be a testimony for others who will follow after us. One life comes to mind, who called out to me from the onset of his life and ministry. This life is that of one of the greatest missionaries of all time ... Hudson Taylor. The first edition of his life story came out in 1918, relating his experiences starting in 1860, roughly 150 years ago. I want to share briefly how his life spoke forward into mine, changing me forever. I had been working with others in a "prayer movement" active in the late 1980's, mobilizing believers to come together to pray for spiritual revival. The flagship verse for the movement was 2 Chronicles 7:14:

> "...if my people, who are called by my name, will humble themselves and pray and seek my face and turn from their wicked ways, then will I hear from heaven and will

forgive their sin and will heal their land."

I was involved with others who were working primarily in the Tacoma-Settle area, but also in communities throughout the state of Washington. In my naïve thinking, it seemed such a simple formula, which could ignite new life into the Lord's Church, as well as restoration to broken, hurting families and self- destructing communities. But it could also set ablaze a concern and movement to reach the "nations" all around us with the gospel, that is the many ethnic groups from all over the world that are immigrants to this region.

"...if my people, who are called by my name, will humble themselves and pray..."

After several years my heart had grown weary with the reality that so few people were taking time out of their schedules to come together and pray for an hour, when the promises of the Bible and the rewards to be experienced for His Kingdom were so worthy of seeking out. My heart was growing more and more discouraged and confused.

I remember well the rainy day I was considering these things in my office, and I just got "fed up" with the weariness and wonderings of these issues. I wanted a respite from the weight of it, and turned to my bookshelf for something to read to take my mind off of my discouragement. My eyes fell upon a rather old and thick volume that I had picked up a few weeks earlier from a large pile in our church entryway ... a place where we in the fellowship would bring the books we no longer wanted or needed, in order to share them with others in the group.

I had hurriedly picked up the book and tucked it into my bag; then upon returning home, I quickly stuck it on my bookshelf as I prepared for guests. I had not even taken a look inside. But this thick, green volume was the very one that caught my eye that memorable gray day amidst the literal gray of a rainy day, and the figurative gray of a weary and discouraged soul. And in this time that I now believe was prepared for me by Papa God, I grabbed the book from my shelf, snuggled up in my bed, and began to read the story of one of the greatest missionaries of all time.

In what seemed like an innocent attempt to occupy a dreary afternoon, a light was sparked in my heart that would burn brighter and brighter to this day ... my life would never be the same. For in those next hours and days I caught the "missions flame" from this one calling back to me from almost a century and a half earlier. The physical and emotional turmoil he had experienced as he strove to fulfill God's call on his life greatly eclipsed my temporary period of discouragement. My heart was hooked.

Anyone who is interested in foreign missions might recognize the name included in the title: *"HUDSON TAYLOR and the China Inland Mission...."*[7] It is a 640 page book, and I'm amazed at the fact that I had picked it up from the table of books in the first place; and in the second place that I had chosen it now, from among dozens in my den. Surely my *hand was in the hand of the one who stills the waters,* to quote in part an old gospel song. And with His hand on my hand and life as I began to devour the story of a most historic life, I had courage and interest to even begin to pick up the torch containing a *"missions flame."*

There is no way that I can adequately express the impact upon my life that this book began to make, as I curled up in my bed and began to digest the meaty stories of this man who opened up inland China to the Christian faith, ultimately bringing thousands into faith in Jesus Christ. I would need to read and quote many passages from the two inch thick volume in my hand at this moment, in order to begin to do justice to the impact of this one life upon mine in those hours. But to summarize only briefly, this courageous man went forth by ship from England to China, then a land barely touched with the gospel of Jesus Christ. He was one of the "firsts" to establish many of the mission paradigms we follow today. One of them was his desire to fit in with the people he was reaching by wearing their native garb. Another was to eat their food with a grateful heart. And yet another was to walk the miles from village to village as the native Chinese did in that day. And it was he who dared to go "beyond the shores" of China to open up the inland areas of China with the gospel message. I could go on to recount many other mission paradigms he influenced.

During his years there he buried at least one wife and more than one child who succumbed to death due to illnesses, some of which we have vaccines for today. He experienced the pain of the "sending" mission group's misunderstanding of these new paradigms and methods he had developed reaching the lost in China. Ultimately the group withdrew support for the mission and sent negative reports to the press and others in his native England. He experienced deprivation of food sources and necessary supplies on some occasions, and serious personal illnesses caused him to spend weeks in bed to reach recovery. Emotional discouragement was also a factor as he pressed deeper into an immense mission field than any others had ever dared to attempt. And the list of his daily challenges and sacrifices could go on and on.

The *purpose in the pain* that came forth is the hallmark of his life. His mission organization, China Inland Mission, was expelled from China during World War II. But even that did not stop the powerful flow of reverberations from his life, as the agency became known as Overseas Missionary Fellowship, and as such began to open up parts of the Philippines and other regions of the world to a fullness of the gospel of Jesus Christ.

As so a little later the life of Hudson Taylor through OMF touched even our lives with a funny sort of "passing the torch" experience, on our very first mission trip almost 20 years ago. My husband, Dave and I spent several days with a couple, who were the Philippine directors of Overseas Missionary Fellowship in Manila, Philippines during that trip. Some things are still clearly imprinted on my memory of our days staying with them, as they shared their life and experiences as long-term missionaries there. A few rather odd remaining memories follow:

- The wife went to visit a young Filipino woman in the hospital who had just delivered her first child. I think my mouth fell open in almost disbelief as she shared how the hospital was so crowded that two new mothers would be assigned to each bed in the maternity ward.

- I remember the trails of the tiniest ants I had ever seen, as they marched on the walls of our small guest room to fetch an even tinier crumb from my toast.

- We took our cold showers, as there was no hot water heater in their humble apartment.

- We visited a village Church in the rural area not far outside of Manila, staying for lunch. After I had eaten and enjoyed several helpings of the tasty, crispy dark-brown substance within the chicken dumplings, I was told it was fried blood.

- We showed "The Jesus Film" in one area, where the mosquitos seemed to outnumber the attendees ten to one.

- We were shocked in unbelief as we saw the numerous one room cardboard and black plastic houses in the "Squatters' Village" lining the city roadway in the heart of Manila.

- We listened with the missionaries on their "short wave" radio to catch the latest news they could get from England.

Looking back at this quaint potpourri of memories from that short experience with these committed and effective long-term missionaries, I smile as the glimpses don't seem so odd now ... but they did then! And in their tiny apartment the Holy Spirit fanned the missions' flame; it was the bedrock experience of countless future mission trips. I thank God for their influence upon our life decisions in that short week, and I will also thank Mr. Taylor for his dynamic impact on our lives when I meet him in heaven, or on the earth if Jesus and he come back to earth before I die.

So, the influence of Hudson Taylor lives on, as in missionary circles he is esteemed as one of the greatest of the greats as we survey the history of modern missions.

Looking down to my desk now at this worn and yellowed, dark green volume with Chinese letters on the front that contains many of his life experiences, suffice it to say that my heart is still moved by it. I remember with pathos how I read chapter after chapter of his book that I had picked up that day so many years ago.

And I have praised God over and over for allowing my gaze and hand to fall upon this priceless treasure in the pile of those books no longer desired or valued by others. I am reminded of a song a contemporary worship leader named Matt Redman has written and sings, with a chorus that pours forth, "Worship is the heart of missions' flame..." It pierces my heart today as I remember how my tired and weary soul, amidst my disappointment and discouragement in one area of ministry, was set ablaze by the testimony of this giant in the field of missions, Hudson Taylor ... causing me to praise God, and changing my life forever. It was not too many months hence that my husband and I answered the call to a short-term mission to South Korea and the Philippines, from which I shared the memories on pages 121-122.

Now nearly 25 years later the dozens of air flights to countries we have touched with the gospel of Jesus Christ are just a blur, too numerous to even remember or recount. And Dave will be taking even more this week as he travels and ministers in several mission fields of Asia, and he carries on with God's mandate on our lives to take the gospel of salvation through Jesus Christ "to the ends of the earth."

I have wondered if Hudson Taylor ever came to understand even in some small measure the "purpose in the pain" that he experienced, and the effect that his life would have on so many others, including mine, even to this very day.

I am reminded of Betsie Ten Boom's last words to her beloved sister Corrie, as she seemed to know that she would not recover from her illness: "...must tell people what we have learned here. We must tell them that there is no pit so deep that He is not deeper still. They will listen to us, Corrie, because we have been here."

Here we see that Betsie made an appraisal of their experience for herself. She determined the purpose behind the pain, and the potential for their lives to affect generations beyond themselves. Little could she have imagined just how many thousands would be impacted in the reading of their story over the ensuing four decades, and book copyrights in 1971, 1984 and 2006, not to mention the movie that was made about their experiences. In reading again the forward to my 2006 copy, I see a more up-to-date appraisal by Joni Eareckson Tada: "...when I would occasionally fall back into my own pit of fear or depression, the Spirit of God would tenderly bring to mind Betsie's well- known phrases: "There is no pit so deep that God's love is not deeper still." And also, "Only heaven will reveal the top side of God's tapestry."

If we don't attempt some appraisal of our difficult times for ourselves, we are vulnerable, and may by default pick up the appraisal of others, which may prove to be false. We need to appraise our situations in the presence of the Holy Spirit who leads us into all truth, as we attempt to understand, even in some small measure ... a purpose in the pain. Yet it is vital to remember that the purpose may not be immediately revealed; it may take months or years until the full retrospective vision of the circumstance is clear enough to see and understand a purpose, even to some measure. Or it could even wait for His face-to-face insight.

Remember the advice in Hebrews 12:2-3:

> *"Let us fix our eyes on Jesus, the author and perfecter of our faith, who for the joy set before Him endured the cross, scorning its shame, and sat down at the right hand of the throne of God. Consider Him who endured*

such opposition from sinful men, so that you will not grow weary and lose heart."

Jesus is our best example of discerning the purpose in the pain, and one who is with us in every "cross-like" experience. Remember, **only Jesus was truly forsaken**. But we also need to remember that we sometimes don't acquire a more heavenly perspective until we look back sometime later.

The Cambodian man, Rev. Setan Lee in chapter eight thought he would become a doctor. But God had other plans for his life. He has returned to Cambodia many times and done much to improve the situation of his countrymen there since the time of his suffering. But even in that, the full purpose had not been revealed. For now, we know he has traveled the world for years, relating his gruesome story and encouraging others with the truth of God's faithfulness in the worst of times. In all of my years, his testimony may prove to be the most powerful I have ever heard. In that weekend when he spoke at the large church fellowship near us, over a thousand people were touched by his testimony. I suspect he will reach many thousands more in the months and years to come with the story of God's faithfulness and love during his unimaginable sufferings. Truly a powerful *doctor of the soul* he has become!

But we also sometimes ask ourselves, "What if we look and pray, and we still don't seem to see a purpose in our pain?" What if the Holy Spirit seems to be quiet ... and the understanding doesn't seem to come to us. We are not alone, for Jesus has gone "deeper still" on our behalf. *"My God, my God, **why** have you forsaken me?"* Matthew 27:46. We don't even begin to understand the perplexity He is describing or wonder at the surprise that He is expressing within the forsaking. But even in the midst of feeling forsaken, He cried out with a loud voice, *"Father, into your hands I commit my spirit"* Luke 23:46.

It is very interesting to note that in the previous verse, Luke 23:45, a purpose in the pain is revealed to the reader: "and the curtain of the temple was torn in two." The note in the margin of my Bible summarizes it wonderfully: *"The curtain between the Holy Place and the Most Holy Place. Its tearing symbolized Christ's opening the way directly to God."* I am so thankful for this concrete visual image God gave to mankind concerning the spirit work Jesus was accomplishing. But it seems Jesus had no way of seeing or knowing of that at the time of His confused and despairing exclamations of Matthew 27:46, above. In His death the curtain of separation between God and man had been torn in two, but only later would He see the full fruit of His horrific, agonizing labors.

Nevertheless, even in His terrible suffering and perceived abandonment by the Father, He committed Himself into the Father's hands. John 19:30a states: *"When He had received the drink, Jesus said, 'it is finished.'"* He had struggled against sin for us and finished His earthly life victoriously. Speaking of His victory over sin, Hebrews 12:3-4 says:

"Consider Him who endured such opposition from sinful men, so that you will not grow weary and lost heart. In your struggle against sin, you have not yet resisted to the point of shedding your blood."

I believe the "finished" Jesus spoke of was this victory of living the sinless life, as no other human had ever done, or would ever do. Yet there was more to be accomplished on our behalf. Let's search a little deeper for the hidden treasure in His words.

"When He had received the drink, Jesus said, 'It is finished.' With that, He bowed His head and gave up His spirit" John 19:30.

The "gave up" here in Greek is "paradidomi" – "to hand over, *deliver to prison*, to entrust, commit, pass on." Jesus gave Himself over to the grave and whatever lay ahead in the three days before He would rise up to the Father. (For in John 20:17, three days after His crucifixion, Jesus spoke to Mary Magdalene in the garden saying, *"Do not hold on to me, for I have not yet returned to the Father. Go instead to my brothers and tell them I am returning to my Father...."*)

In Matthew 27:50 it says of Jesus' death, *"And when Jesus had cried out again in a loud voice, He gave up His spirit."* Interestingly, the Greek word used here for "gave up" is a slightly different one. It is "aphiemi," which means *"to abandon,* forgive, pardon, remit, cancel, to leave, to allow, permit, tolerate, forgive." The first key word here is "abandon," for I believe He abandoned Himself into the Father's hands, not knowing exactly what these three days would hold. In Matthew 12:40 Jesus prophesied, "For as Jonah was three days and three nights in the belly of a huge fish, so the son of Man will be three days and three nights in the heart of the earth." He knew this time was coming, and yet He abandoned Himself into the next phase of His suffering, whatever that might be. And in that place He would continue the work necessary for the Father to *"pardon, remit, cancel and forgive"* the sins of all mankind for all of time. Hebrews 10:10 states, *"And by that will, we have been made holy through the sacrifice of the body of Jesus Christ once for all."*

To summarize a point, in Matthew 27:46 Jesus cries out to the Father, asking, *"...why have you forsaken me?"* Nevertheless, a short time later Jesus breathed His last, saying, *"Father, into your hands I commit my spirit"* Luke 23:46. In not seeing any apparent answer to His *"why"* question, Jesus was yet able to "commit" His spirit into the hands of the Father He trusted, for whatever lay ahead. In the middle of *"nevertheless"* is where we find our example and our hope ... when we can't seem to find the purpose in the pain, suffering, loss, abandonment, or grief we are experiencing. Jesus has been there for us; He has been *deeper still*, and He can experience it with us in the moments of our questionings and almost endless wonderings. And by His grace we can trust in the Father's loving omnipotence and omniscience, just as He did.

"And He is the head of the body, the Church; He is the beginning and the firstborn from among the dead, so that in everything He might have the supremacy. For God was pleased to have all His fullness dwell in Him, and through Him to reconcile to Himself all things, whether things on earth or things in heaven, by making peace through His blood, shed on the cross" Colossians 1:18-20.

From this "deepest place" of suffering on the cross and in the following three days, where many believe He actually endured unimaginable sufferings in hell for our sins and sicknesses, He came forth victoriously.

But whether He rose from the grave, or from hell itself, He still came forth victoriously, to take His place with the Father, having finished His work on our behalf as He *"took up our infirmities...carried our sorrows...was pierced for our transgressions...and crushed for our iniquities"* Isaiah 53:4-5.

And from the place of His resurrection to be united again with the Father, He sent to us His Holy Spirit, who helps us and prays for us in our times of need.

"...the Spirit helps us in our weakness. We do not know what we ought to pray for, but the Spirit himself intercedes for us with groans that words cannot express. And He who searches our hearts knows the mind of the Spirit, because the Spirit intercedes for the saints in accordance with God's will" Romans 8:26-27.

From the **deepest place** beneath the sins and sicknesses of all humanity for all time, He rose to take His place in the **highest place** at the right hand of the Father in heaven.

"*Therefore, God exalted Him to the **highest place** and gave Him the name that is above every name, that at the name of Jesus every knee should bow, in heaven and on earth and under the earth, and every tongue confess that Jesus Christ is Lord, to the glory of God the Father*" Philippians 2:8-11.

"*But we have this treasure in jars of clay to show that this all-surpassing power is from God and not from us. **We are hard pressed on every side, but not crushed; perplexed, but not in despair; persecuted, but not abandoned; struck down, but not destroyed.** We always carry around in our body the death of Jesus, so that the life of Jesus may also be revealed in our body. For we who are alive are always being given over to death for Jesus' sake, so that His life may be revealed in our mortal body.*" 2 Corinthians 4:7-11.

We see that Paul saw the purpose of his pain being manifest through his life, and through his words he encourages those who will follow in his footsteps to embrace a deeper purpose – that purpose being to reveal the life and power of Jesus Christ our Lord to a waiting and watching world ... a world desperate for lives of wholeness, meaning and significance.

"Through Jesus, therefore, let us continually offer to God a sacrifice of praise – the fruit of lips that confess His name. And do not forget to do good and to share with others, for with such sacrifices God is pleased."

Hebrews 13:15-16

Chapter Twelve

I Will Yet Praise Him

As we draw nearer to the end of this book, my heart recognizes that we have gone along many winding paths into recesses containing some small measure of understanding into the subject of suffering in one form or another. But I find myself looking for some word from the Lord to sort of sum things up. And I believe Psalm 42:1-3 will do that to some extent.

> *"As the deer pants for streams of water, so my soul pants for you O God. My soul thirsts for God, for the living God. When can I go and meet with God? My tears have been my food day and night, while men say to me all day long, 'Where is your God?' "*

God sometimes seems afar off in the midst of our circumstances, and even our friends or family don't seem to fully understand the emotional, physical or spiritual state we are in. When we have been open about our faith in God in the past, this question, "Where is your God?" is often hinted at or even blatantly asked by those who don't understand that the presence of God in our life doesn't automatically make it "a bowl of cherries." It is a part of the human experience to ask *ourselves* even, "Where is God?" If we feel somewhat abandoned by Him within the place of disappointment or suffering, and we have lost the sense of His presence within it, we may be asking literally, "Where is

God?" Or if we are convinced of His presence, even though we don't seem to sense it acutely, our hearts may really be asking, "Where is God in *this circumstance?*" "What is He trying to say or do in this circumstance in my life ... or perhaps in the lives of others who look on?"

Psalm 42:4 goes on to say, *"These things I remember as I pour out my soul ..."* Like the tiny dot on the paper, made by the sharp end of a protractor as we draw a circle, this very short statement contains such a poignant and precise place to start in seeing the bigger picture (or circle), and yielding to God the rights to fill in the details making up the contents of it. It is in this place of pondering, wondering, and even asking God for some purpose behind it, that we can *"pour out our souls"* to Him ... for He alone knows how deeply we long for the cries of our hearts to be heard, and He alone has the deeper level of compassion and understanding that we are desiring. Jesus experienced the deepest level of suffering and abandonment on the cross, yet within His agony, His last cry was still, *"Father, into Your hands I commit my spirit"* Luke 23:46.

As we pour out our memories, thoughts, and emotions to the Lord, our experience is often much like that of the psalmist, "... how I *used to go* with the multitude, leading the procession to the house of God, with shouts of thanksgiving among the festive throng" Psalm 42:4b. We tend to remember the "better days," when we used to do things we can't do now, either due to lack of proximity or finances, decreased physical or mental capacity, absence of friends or colleague who used to accompany us, loss of employment or status, and a myriad of other reasons or situations.

A wise man has often reminded me of a point of good theology, yet very poor grammar ... so poor it seems to help make the point of his thought: "God ain't nervous." When he has repeated this phrase to me, he has done so to remind me that God isn't surprised or offended when we pour out to Him the deepest things of our hearts ... our disappointments, sorrows, questions, concerns, dreams; and even our dissatisfaction with Him in allowing these disappointing and difficult things to be a part of our lives.

Hebrews chapter eleven reminds us of the "greats" of the faith in the Bible, and yet as we read it we can remember things about their walk that weren't really stellar or worthy of imitation. David, who wrote many of the Psalms is one example. Like us, he had his times of failure, and lapses in his obedience to the known will of God. And yet we have these awesome chapters available to read, and they almost serve as a *template* upon which we can pour out our own souls to God. Sometimes when Dave and I start our daily morning prayer and Bible study time together, I open up to the Psalms and start to read one. This is almost a "flag" to him that I am experiencing some sort of emotional, physical or spiritual challenge, and I need to let the words of the psalmist help me express my emotions and heart to God.

In Psalm 42 verse 5b we see a ray of hope when the psalmist seems to talk to himself, *"Put your hope in God, for I shall yet praise Him, for the help of His countenance* (NKJV)." Verse six goes on to say, *"My soul is downcast within me; therefore I will remember you from the land of the Jordan, the heights of Hermon – from Mount Mizar."* My Bible notes suggest that the Psalmist could possibly be speaking from a place of exile outside the contemporary boundaries of Israel and Judah. If we look more closely at these places, we can see that he is purposely looking back to times when God had shown Himself powerful on their behalf, or given them comfort and solace. In Deuteronomy 4:48 we see that when the Israelites came out of Egypt, Hermon was the place of northernmost victory for the Israelites, as they took the land. And Genesis 13:10 says of Jordan, "...the whole plain of the Jordan was well watered like the garden of the Lord." It seems that his purposeful act of reminding himself of these more positive circumstances reinforces the paradigm of "praise precedes deliverance" that we discussed earlier.

And it reminds me again of the earlier stellar example of this truth, where in Acts 16 we read of Paul and Silas being seized, dragged, flogged, and thrown into prison with their feet in the stocks ... all of this because they had healed the fortune-telling slave girl and removed her owner's ability to make money by her. In verse 22 we read that in this condition, they were praying and singing hymns to God around midnight. God brought forth an earthquake which freed them from their bondage, and

134

ultimately resulted in the salvation of the jailer and his whole household.

If you find your heart is moved to understand more about this paradigm, "praise precedes deliverance," I want to recommend the book *Hallelujah Factor*[6] by Jack Taylor, who is an excellent tutor on it. Moving on to Psalm 42:7, we read,

"**Deep** *calls to* **deep** *in the roar of your waterfalls; all you waves and breakers have swept over me.*"

In this deep place, which he describes as like the noise and dizziness of waves wildly overwhelming him, feeling crushed down and swept about, his soul cries out from its depth, and pushes in even further to call to the things of God that are deeper still. Verse 8 in the New King James Version describes how God meets him in his circumstances:

"*The Lord will command His loving-kindness in the daytime, and in the night His song shall be with me – a prayer to the God of my life.*"

It seems that in the wakeful times in the night, the enemy likes to sneak in and attempt to throw over us his wet blanket of discouragement and fear.

"*My bones suffer mortal agony as my foes taunt me, saying to me all day (and night) long, 'Where is your God?'* " Psalm 42:10.

In this place, is it so helpful to literally remember *His song* in the night.

I tend to have these periods of wakefulness fairly often, and I am familiar with the attempts of the enemy to drag down my spirits and give me anxiety about the day to come. Therefore, I have purposed to apply the strategies I have been speaking about. Next to my bed is a small CD player, equipped with a CD of praise and worship. Tuned in to a low volume so as not to awaken my husband, I begin to praise and worship God, dispelling the accusations and lies of the enemy with the truths of the presence, personality, power and victory of God.

Many of the songs that I have chosen are taken directly from the Word of God, for the Word itself has power to dispel the darkness of fear or despair. When I was a young girl I took piano lessons for a time, and one song I learned to play quite well was, "Standing on the Promises." One phrase I still remember goes, *"Standing on the promises of Christ my King; to eternal ages let His praises ring, standing on the promises of God."* I remember a scene from the movie, *"The Hiding Place"* where Betsie ten Boom would in the evenings in the barracks of the prison camp, take out her most prized possession, the tiny New Testament that she and her sister Corrie had miraculously smuggled into the camp. And in the place of pain, sickness, exhaustion, fleas, lice, overcrowding and discouragement ... she would pour forth upon the thirsty crowd around her the living water of the Word of God, and others would find encouragement and hope – for the promises of His presence amidst their suffering, and His promises of eternal life beyond that horrid place where so many were dying daily.

This experience reminds me so poignantly of the importance of the Word of God laid down in our lives early in the morning, late at night, and throughout the day and night as the Holy Spirit allows and directs our times. It was the life-blood for these prisoners, and it can be our life-preserver of hope and reality, when we see ourselves falling into any deep places of misfortune, discouragement, pain, trouble, suffering, confusion or despair.

Standing *on His promises beats* *struggling* *beneath the circumstances.*

And in the concluding verse of Psalm 42 the psalmist declares again his intent to praise God amidst his circumstances: "Why are you downcast, O my soul? Why so disturbed within me? Put your hope in God, for *I will yet praise Him*, my Savior and my God."

In the New Testament Peter gives us some awesome advice in 1 Peter 4:19:

"Therefore let those who suffer according to the will of God commit their souls to Him in doing good, as to a faithful creator" 1 Peter 4:19.

And our Lord Jesus perfected the thought:

"Father, into Your hands I commit my spirit" Luke 23:46b.

"But we know that when He appears, we shall be like Him, for we shall see Him as He is. Everyone who has this hope in Him purifies himself, just as He is pure."

1 John 3:2b-3

"And just as we have borne the likeness of the earthly man, so shall we bear the likeness of the man from heaven."

1 Corinthians 15:49

Chapter Thirteen

He Is Coming Soon

As I bring this study to a close, there is one more concept that I want to hold before our hearts and minds, to be considered in the power and revelation of the Holy Spirit. This short paragraph from Joni Eareckson Tada's forward to the newest edition of *The Hiding Place* introduces it so wonderfully.

> *"You can understand why, when I first met Corrie ten Boom, I was filled with glee. She grasped my shoulder firmly and announced in her thick Dutch accent, 'Oh Joni, it will be a grand day when we will dance together in heaven!' The image she painted of us skipping down streets of gold left me breathless. I could easily picture the scene of glory and gladness. It made me realize I had survived."*[8]

From this place of her advanced age, it was heaven and our hope of new bodies that Corrie was seeing as she met Joni that day, her body paralyzed from her accident earlier in life. Surely, we are given good Biblical evidence to support her encouraging words.

> *"Dear friends, now we are children of God, and what we will be has not yet been made known. But we know that when He appears, we shall be like Him, for we shall see Him as He is"* 1 John 3:2.

"And just as we have borne the likeness of the earthly man, so shall we bear the likeness of the man from heaven" 1Corinthians 15:49.

In this day and age some are indeed taking on a new perspective of hope and possibility. For instance, in the church fellowship we attend, a young couple have two young children who both have a rare and yet incurable disease that is robbing them of their ability to walk and use their arms normally. And for them the hope of a new body within their lifetime is a reality, if Jesus doesn't bring healing to them before His return.

I don't need to list for you all of the many "end times" fulfillments from Revelations that have already come to pass in the past ten to twenty years. But to consider a few, we could look at the dizzying increase in incidence of earthquakes, floods, devastating forest fires, draught and famine, and other natural catastrophes taking place. We could point to the wars, recent overthrows of a number of world governments, and many other global events that cause some of us to wonder just how deep into "the seals" of Revelation Chapter 6 we may already be, even now. We don't need to itemize many more signs of the times in order to begin to ponder the fact that those of us reading this book at this moment could possibly be among those in the "last generation" upon planet earth as we know it.

My husband and I are so convinced of it that when we are speaking we sometimes shock people with our statement, "We don't expect to die." People are aghast, wondering how we could have bodies that are invincible. Then we explain how soon we feel the Lord's appearing will be, even before the end of our lives. We truly are living our lives in such a way that we prepare ourselves and attempt to prepare others to endure the tribulation that the scriptures describe for those "last days." And even if there is a "rapture" that removes God's people from the worst events of the tribulation, as many believe, there is a measure that must be suffered in advance of it and is already being suffered by so many faithful saints upon the earth today.

We know many Christian leaders who, like us, are even now beginning to make physical preparations for that time of tribulation, whether it contains a rapture in advance of the worst sufferings, or a rapture to meet Jesus in the air at the time of His second coming through the clouds to take up His earthly reign.

We believe there is a comfort that can be experienced by those currently facing tribulations, suffering, debilitating diseases or conditions such as Joni triumphs through. And that is the hope that, after all the many generations who have lived upon planet earth, we are among those living in the last few, if not the very last generation ... before His grand appearing, when the disabilities and sufferings are cast aside, and our bodies are made new.

From pulpits around the world, to many books in the Bible bookstores, to guest speakers on *God TV*, to the revelations of *Revelation*, to the move of the Holy Spirit in our own hearts...

the truth of His soon coming is becoming a reality to a multitude.

"Dear Friends, now we are children of God, and what we will be has not yet been made known. But we know that when He appears, we shall be like Him, for we shall see Him as He is" 1 John 3:2.

"And just as we have borne the likeness of the earthly man, so shall we bear the likeness of the man from heaven"
1 Corinthians 15:49.

We want to remember that Jesus is the Alpha and Omega, the beginning and the end. He knows all things; He has created all things and is within all things. And no matter how deep these things might take us before His return, **Jesus is "deeper still."**

I am reminded of a question asked me recently. If you are approaching a closed door through which you have passed many times, when will you put up your hand to grasp the door knob? Will you wait until your feet are a few inches from the door? Or will your hand begin to come up to grasp the doorknob several steps before you arrive at the door?

That's how close we are today to the doorway to eternity – either to heaven, or to the millennial renewal of the earth. How will we prepare?

"For here we do not have an enduring city, but we are looking for the city that is to come. Through Jesus, therefore, let us continually offer to God a sacrifice of praise – the fruit of lips that confess His name. And

do not forget to do good and to share with others, for with such sacrifices God is pleased" Hebrews 13:14-16.

Footnotes

[1] Ten Boom, Corrie with Elizabeth and John Sherrill. *The Hiding Place*, Grand Rapids, Michigan: Chosen Books, 2006, p.7-9.

[2] Ibid., p. 227.

[3] Woodrum, David C., *Kingdom Exploration, Restoring Our Understanding of the Gospel of the Kingdom of God,* Chehalis, Washington: Preparing the Way Publishers, 2012.

[4] "*2010 Copiapo Mining Accident*", Wikipedia Encyclopedia, November, 2011.

[5] Setan Lee, Setan A, Randa Lee with Shelba Hammond, *Miracles in the Forgotten Land and Beyond*, Xulon Press, 2010.

[6] Taylor, Jack, *Hallelujah Factor*, Kingdom Publishing, Revised, 1999.

[7] Taylor, Dr. and Mrs. Howard, *Hudson Taylor and the China Inland Mission*, London: The China Inland Mission, 1918-1943.

[8] Ten Boom, Corrie with Elizabeth and John Sherrill. *The Hiding Place*, Grand Rapids, Michigan: Chosen Books, 2006, p. 8.

Other Books By
Janice Woodrum

Hope to Hear...Soon

This Fiery Love

Cherish Life! A Biography of Sarah Palin and Family

Meet me in the Garden

About The Author

Janice Woodrum is a retired Registered Nurse, and a writer who began to minister part-time in 1988, and in 1991 answered a Holy Spirit call to full-time ministry. Together, she and her husband David worked in prayer and revival ministry for years. In 1994 they founded Harvest of Jubilee Groups, Int'l., a Christian missionary organization headquartered in Tacoma, Washington, USA. Harvest of Jubilee is presently affiliated with ministry efforts in 29 countries, primarily throughout Asia and Africa. They typically travel several times a year providing relational oversight, while sponsoring leadership conferences and evangelistic healing miracle events. Beginning in 1997, they developed a copyright-free, Bible College curriculum which presently includes several 6-month Continuing Education CERTIFICATE courses, a 1-year DIPLOMA Program; a 2-year ASSOCIATE Degree in Christian Ministry & Missions Development, and a 4-year BACHELOR of Divinity. This curriculum is provided without expense to the recipients. Janice wrote 29 articles for Diabetes Self-Management Magazine from 1986 - 2000. Since then she has authored several Christian 'faith-development' books. Additionally, she is the Academic Dean and the Director of Curriculum Development for Harvest of Jubilee School of Prayer & Missions.

Janice presently holds a: Doctorate of Theology in Leadership; Master of Theology in Worship and Prayer; Master of Ministry; and a Bachelor of Science in Nursing -with special honors from the University of Colorado.

She and her husband David live on a small 10-acre farm in Chehalis, Washington. Together they have 5 children who are each married. They are blessed with 17 grandchildren.

Harvest of Jubliee Groups, International
hojspm@juno.com

About The Cover

The cover of this book is designed to depict a long, dark tunnel into "the depths of the earth," or the depths of our own human experience – the "deep pit" of Betsie ten Boom's profound statement, "There is no pit so deep that He is not deeper still." He comes toward us from the "deeper still" depth of this deepest place, with arms of love and acceptance out-stretched.

We see that this tunnel or shaft appears on the right to possibly have been constructed with man-made, hewn brick-like stones, such as an ancient waterway or sewer might have been made. Yet on the other side it appears to have been hewn out of the earth itself.

This contrast reminds me that sometimes the difficult places in which we might find ourselves are in part due to our own making – bad judgments, poor choices, or failure to obey the principles of God that we know. And yet, often our deepest and darkest situations are not directly related to our choices or performance. They are related to the fact that we live in a fallen world – one that is progressing rapidly to the conclusion of it, as we know it.

"Bad things do happen to good people," so to speak. And yet it is only natural and human to wonder into the "why" of it, or "whose fault is it anyway?" But in either case, our God, the Lord Jesus Christ, comes forth victoriously as an instrument of light, hope and life.

Jesus is quoted as saying in John 12:46:

"I have come as a light into the world, that whoever believes in me should not abide in darkness." NKJV

We are on a journey and quest to learn to trust more and more in His sovereignty and presence within our life circumstances. Psalm 24:1 says it clearly:

"The earth is the Lord's and everything in it, the world and all who live in it."

And even within the darkest of circumstances that the enemy of our souls has meant for evil, Jesus is there, and can use them for our good.

"And we know that in all things God works for the good of those who love Him, who have been called according to His purpose. For those God foreknew He also predestined to be conformed to the likeness of His Son, that He might be the firstborn among many brothers" Rom. 8:28-29.

A wise friend has encouraged me often with the true statement, "God is often more interested in our character than our comfort."

In the cover we surprisingly see living plants along the seemingly dark path – a visual image of His ability as the *Light of the World* to bring life, new growth and sustenance out of the darkest places in which we may find ourselves.

The deep blue of the cover background is representative of His royalty as King of Kings and Lord of Lords – holy, sovereign, and all-powerful.

The picture, taken as a whole, is designed to give us a lasting mental image to hold onto: "No matter how deep and dark is the pit we may find ourselves in, we need to be looking and listening for the light and voice of the presence of the all-powerful and ever-present One, coming to meet us where we are, with arms of acceptance and love outstretched.

149

My sincere thanks to our son, Steve Woodrum for the artistic cover development.

Made in the USA
Columbia, SC
05 August 2019